Great Empires, Small Nations

Large empires and small nations, rather than "sovereign" states, are the pillars for expanding freedom, democracy and well-being in the current world. The steady increase in the number of small independent countries, as well as the broad self-government of other communities – including, for instance, Bavaria, Catalonia, Flanders, Kashmir, Quebec and Scotland, among many others – relies upon the operation of vast democratic empires, such as the United States of America and the European Union. It is the provision of large-scale public goods, especially defense, security, trade agreements, common currencies and communication networks, that make a small nation viable without its own army, borders or customs.

The traditional West European model of state has largely failed elsewhere and is in decline even where it originated. The European states have achieved stable peace and prosperity only when they have built a large, democratic and free-market "empire." Most of North America, Russia and Asia has never followed the model of sovereign state, while in Latin America, Africa and the Arab region, the failure of a high number of states is unquestionable.

Democracy does not require sovereign states. According to the most recent European experience and the American one before, the building of large military and commercial empires appears to be a condition for stability and progress, as well as an opportunity for small nations' democratic self-government.

Colomer's book is a stimulating read, certainly for anyone willing to entertain nonconventional observations that hold up well on what is happening in the world. I expect this book to be widely read and greatly admired.
Sidney Weintraub, William E. Simon Chair in Political Economy, Center for Strategic and International Studies, Washington DC.

Great Empires, Small Nations is an original and persuasive book. Colomer looks beyond nation–states and discovers the world that does not resemble the Westphalian paradigm. The book makes an important contribution to our understanding of international politics, especially in Europe.
Jan Zielonka, Professor of European Politics and Ralf Dahrendorf Fellow, University of Oxford.

This book strengthens intellectually what practice shows: that the small nations not only are viable as identities, societies and economies, but can attain excellent performance. This is on provision that they do not confine themselves, but rather participate in great political and economic spaces. Besides its intellectual quality, this book has another great merit: it opens gates to hope, something we need in Catalonia now. And it does it with solid and consistent arguments, that is, with rationality, some of which it is also convenient for us to have.
Jordi Pujol, President of Catalonia (1980–2003) and President of the Assembly of European Regions (1992–96).

Josep M. Colomer is a member by election of the *Academia Europaea* and a life member of the American Political Science Association. He is currently a Research Professor in Barcelona, Catalonia, Spain, Europe.

D0061078

Great Empires, Small Nations

The uncertain future of the
sovereign state

Josep M. Colomer

Routledge
Taylor & Francis Group

LONDON AND NEW YORK

First published 2007 by Routledge
2 Park Square, Milton Park, Abingdon, Oxon OX14 4RN

Simultaneously published in the USA and Canada
by Routledge
270 Madison Avenue, New York, NY 10016

*Routledge is an imprint of the Taylor & Francis Group, an informa
business*

© 2007 Josep M. Colomer

Typeset in Sabon by Keyword Group Ltd
Printed and bound in Great Britain by Antony Rowe Ltd,
Chippenham, Wiltshire

British Library Cataloguing in Publication Data
A catalogue record for this book is available from the British Library

Library of Congress Cataloging in Publication Data
Colomer, Josep Maria.
  Great empires, small nations: the uncertain future of the sovereign
  state/Josep M. Colomer.
    p. cm
  Includes bibliographical references and index.
  1. National state. 2. State, The. 3. Autonomy. 4. Democracy. I. Title.
  JC311.C627 2007
  320.1–dc22
  2007007164

ISBN 10: 0-415-43774-1 (hbk)
ISBN 10: 0-415-43775-X (pbk)
ISBN 10: 0-203-94604-9 (ebk)

ISBN 13: 978-0-415-43774-5 (hbk)
ISBN 13: 978-0-415-43775-2 (pbk)
ISBN 13: 978-0-203-94604-6 (ebk)

Summary

"A small community's self-government is nowadays feasible without an army, borders or customs, that is, without a sovereign state."

"It is the large-scale markets and public goods provided by vast empires that make small nations viable."

"There is no such thing as 'globalization,' but rather several market areas of 'imperial' size."

"Small nations develop higher proportions of international trade than large ones."

"With transnational economic integration, regional specialization and differentiation increase."

"Most people of the world are plurilingual."

"Traditional European-style states are too small for security, trade and communications, and too large for democratic self-government."

"Small nations are more democratic than large ones; among large states, federations are much more democratic than those that are centralized."

"Most of North America, Russia and Asia have been unacquainted with the Westphalian, European model of sovereign states."

"In many cases in Africa, Latin America and the Arab region, the very idea of 'state' is frustrated since governments have not attained an internal monopoly nor external sovereignty."

"The American foreign affairs doctrine postulates democratization as the best way to international peace, but democracy does not require sovereign states."

"Peace-making in the Middle East would be more successful with the establishment of an Arab Union promoting cooperation on common economic and security purposes."

"The present United States is a kind of democratic empire without imperialists."

"The European Union is also a democratic empire: expanding outwards, territorially diverse, with multilevel governance."

"Transfrontier cooperation between regional and local governments has overcome the sovereignty of European states."

"In Europe and other imperial areas, the actual difference between small nations' formal independence and their autonomy is a question of degree."

"According to the most recent European experience and the American one before, the building of military and commercial large 'empires' appears to be a condition for stability and progress."

Contents

Tables

Introduction

The imperial opportunity for small nations

The present world offers hitherto unknown opportunities for small nations' self-government. The opportunities for small nations are strongly linked to the operation of vast democratic empires, such as the United States of America and the European Union. It is the large-scale public goods provided by vast empires that make a small nation viable without having to form a sovereign state.

The "small nation" category, as it will be defined and used here, includes formally independent countries in Europe such as Ireland, Estonia, Latvia, Lithuania, or Slovenia, which would hardly be viable outside a large empire; official "lands" or "regions," such as Bavaria, Catalonia, Flanders, Piedmont, or Scotland, within large federal-type states; and hundreds of other countries with disparate official statuses in other parts of the world, from Kashmir to Palestine or Quebec. Traditional empires like China, or other areas of comparable magnitude, might also liberate small nations if they became sufficiently efficient in providing large-scale public goods and liberalized themselves. In the rest of the world, emerging nations and failed states could also be more successful if they were able to build vast "imperial"-sized networks to serve common economic, security and communication interests.

Three worldwide processes affecting the "size" of viable, efficient and democratic political units are identified and put in relation in this book. First, the number of independent and autonomous countries tends to increase, leading to an overall decrease in the size of countries. While there were only about 50 independent countries in the world at the beginning of the twentieth century, there are nearly 200 members of the United Nations in the early twenty-first century. Additionally, more than 500 small governments with elected legislative assemblies exist within vast empires or large federal states.

Second, the number of democracies also increases, having more than doubled in the last thirty years. Small countries are democratic in a much higher proportion than large states. In a world with a very high number of small political units, since the end of the twentieth century, and for first time in history, most human beings live under democratic or liberal regimes.

Third, the traditional larger states forfeit decision-making powers on issues that had founded their external sovereignty and internal monopoly to both great empires and small nations. At the same time, the number of failed, nominally "sovereign" but in fact isolated states, increases in different parts of the world.

Taking the picture as a whole, the increase in the number of viable small democratic governments seems to rely upon membership of very large areas of "imperial" size, which provide public goods such as defense, security, trade agreements, common currencies and communication networks – as is analyzed in the second part of this book. While a number of large sovereign states, especially in Western Europe, had been able to maintain territorial control and provide certain public goods with relative efficiency, the development of new transport and communication technologies has enlarged the scope of feasible human exchanges. Within efficient, internally varied great empires, small nations are now viable and, at the same time, better fitted than large, heterogeneous states for democratic self-government.

As a paramount case of these worldwide processes, in the third part of this book the European Union is analyzed as an "empire." The European Union is a very large political unit that has expanded continuously outwards, is organized diversely across the territory, and has multiple, overlapping institutional levels of governance. It has adopted Europe-wide common democratic institutions and has made democracy a flagship for its member states. But with transnational economic integration, regional specialization and differences increase across Europe, promoting a growing demand for small units' self-government. In fact, more than 200 regional and local governments have permanent diplomatic delegations in Brussels, separate from member states, to deal directly with the institutions of the European Union.

Participation of small nations' governments in the institutions of the European Union, as well as transfrontier cooperation between regional and local governments, is persistently eroding the sovereignty of traditional European states. This does not necessarily prelude a dramatic breaking point, but rather a steady process by which the difference between formal independence and autonomy for small nations will be merely a question of degree. A small community's self-government is nowadays possible without having its own army, borders or customs, that is, without having a sovereign state.

Western Europe was the historical scene of modern nation–state building, a model that has either not been applied or has mostly failed elsewhere in the world. Now the validity of the traditional West European model of sovereign nation–state has weakened even further because it is in decline even in the original experience. It is large empires and small nations that can be, in contrast, the pillars for expanding freedom, democracy and well-being in the current world. Somehow Europe appears again as a possible reference model for building efficient and democratic political units in other parts of the world, but, in contrast to the former homogenizing model of nation–states, the current European imperial model involves territorial diversity and democracy at multiple levels.

Plan of the book

This book is classified as a "non-fiction essay," which means that it seeks to be readable in a comfortable way. The following pages are not those of an academic treatise, but rather a collection of facts, hypotheses, opinions and well-grounded statements proven elsewhere. It even contains a few notes in an informal tone and light ironic comments. There are no footnotes; sources and bibliographic references are given at the end, in a separate appendix, in order not to interrupt the reader's flow. However, the academic rules of the game should never be broken because they are, above all, safeguards against deception or tricks. As I myself have summarized elsewhere, any serious piece of work in the social sciences should specify: 1) definitions and classification, 2) quantification, 3) causal hypothesis, and 4) theory.

Accordingly, in this book:

- The fundamental concepts – empire, state and nation – are duly defined in the first part. All political units in the history of the world are classified, on the basis of these definitions, in Tables 1.1, 2.1 and 3.1.
- This allows a quantification of the cases fitting each of the categories, as well as to establish temporal tendencies and regional focuses.
- Changes in the size and other defining characteristics of political units, that is, the prevalence of either empires or states or nations in different historical periods, are hypothesized to derive from two factors. First, they are fostered by technological changes, especially regarding war, transport and communication; consistently, the historical surveys that are presented for different subjects begin at different moments relative to crucial technological innovations. Second, institutional changes are produced by human decisions favoring security, freedom and well-being, such as can be provided by modern electoral democracies.
- Theoretical support for the analysis comes from the economic concept of social efficiency (which relies on the aggregation of individual benefits and costs), from the theory of public goods, and from an emphasis on the role of institutions in defining the territorial areas in which markets can develop, democracy can be exerted and public goods can be provided.

As tentative and provisional as a number of statements in the following pages may be, they are nevertheless submitted to the test of further observations. Almost everything that is held in this book would be wrong if the following things happened during the next few decades: the number of independent or autonomous political units in the world decreased, the number of democratic governments also decreased, and the number of successful large states – defined as a sovereign and monopolistic form of government – increased. Regarding the case of Europe, the hypotheses put forth in this book should also be called into question if the European Union were to be dissolved, interstate military rivalries were to re-emerge or the euro were abandoned. My bet is on a widely diffused process of blurring the differences between formal autonomy and independence for small nations within the European Union – a model which may replicate itself across the rest of the world.

September 11, 2006

Acknowledgements

The first edition of this book, published in Catalan, received the 9th Ramon Trias Fargas Award for Essays 2005. For the Catalan and the Spanish editions I acknowledge Juan M. Atutxa, Xavier Batalla, Joaquim Colominas, Isidor Cònsul, Maria Rosa Fortuny, Carles Gasòliba, Jorge Herralde, Daniel Innerarity, Francisco Jorquera, Enric Juliana, Ignacio Lago, Paul Preston, Vicenç Villatoro, and Antoni Vives. I welcomed helpful comments and corrections from Peter A. Kraus, Roberto Lago, and Josep M. Vallès, which have been taken into account for the present edition. I am also thankful for support from Jordi Pujol, Sidney Weintraub, Jan Zielonka and Routledge editor Craig Fowlie.

Part I

Empires, states and nations

The numerous and very diverse forms of government that have existed in the history of humankind or currently exist can be grouped into three very general categories: empires, states, and nations. There have always been large empires, increasingly large, in fact, as new transport and communication technologies have developed. Most of the world's population lives today within these empires. Sovereign states, in contrast, succeeded in Europe within a historical period that began about 300 years ago and is today essentially finished. Finally, small political units with high degrees of autonomy or independence, including ancient and medieval cities and, in modern times, political "nations," have always been a basic form of collective organization in human history. The main reason for small communities' persistence is that, on the basis of high levels of social homogeneity, they can adopt soft or democratic forms of government with some ease. As a result of these tendencies, the present world is characterized by the broadness and inclusiveness of a few great empires, the decline or failure of sovereign states, and the flourishing of hundreds of small, politically autonomous or independent communities and nations.

1 Large empires

The notion of "empire" can account for more than two dozen cases of ancient, medieval, modern, and current experiences of human government. The ancient Chinese and Persian empires, the classical Roman Empire, the colonial empires of Spain, Britain and France, the modern Russia, and the present configurations of the United States of America and of the European Union, among others that are listed in Table 1.1 at the end of this chapter, share important defining characteristics. These can be summarized as follows:

- *Very large size, in terms of both territory and population.*
- *Absence of fixed or permanent boundaries.* Empires tend to expand over the territory, up to the point of conflict with other empires, and when in decline they may also contract. When an empire is organized on the basis of a large island or archipelago (like present-day Japan, for instance) its territorial borders may remain stable for relatively long periods. But, in general, "territory" should not be considered a strong defining element of empire.
- *A compound of diverse groups and territorial units.* In ancient and medieval times, an empire could be comprised of cities, republics, counties, principalities, bishoprics, and other varied forms of political organization. Today, multiethnic federations can be arranged with less heterogeneous institutional regimes. But democratic empires may also include political units organized with different forms of parliamentary or presidential, unichamber or multichamber, monarchical or republican governments. They may be linked to the center by diverse institutional formulas.
- *A set of multilevel, often overlapping jurisdictions.* Within an empire, no authority typically rules with exclusive powers. Rather, the central government may rule indirectly through local governments; the latter develop self-government on important issues; and power sharing is widespread.

These essential characteristics of the "imperial" form of government – very large size, no fixed boundaries, territorial diversity and multilevel jurisdictions – contrast with the essential characteristics of the "state" and "nation" forms of government that will be discussed in the following chapters.

We should not confound "empire" with "imperialism." While imperialism is a "policy," empire is used here as a "polity" or form of political community. In fact there are empires which are not imperialistic, including, for instance, the Holy Roman and German empire and the present European Union, while some non-imperial but rather homogeneous and centralized states have developed imperialist policies, including Britain, France, Germany and other European nation–states, in this way creating colonial empires.

"Empire" should not be confounded with "dictatorship" either. There have indeed been a number of famous emperors who concentrated and exerted power by dictatorial means, including, for instance, Alexander in the Persian Empire or Genghis Khan in the Mongol empire, although these were not by far among the most durable empires. Actually, some of the most brutal and oppressive empires of modern times, such as Napoleon's France or Hitler's Germany, blatantly failed in very brief spans of time, largely as a consequence of their own extreme levels of power concentration and arbitrary decision making.

In contrast, certain empires with republican forms of government have in the past only delegated power to a temporary dictator in the face of emergency situations, as was originally the case with the Roman Caesars. Other softer and more lasting empires emerged as confederations of previously existing and largely respected political units on which a new central power was superposed, in this manner giving way to new imperial titles such as "king of kings," "supreme king" or "maharaja of rajas." In the Holy Roman and German empire, founded by Charlemagne, the emperor was chosen by a college of grand electors from the largest units, whilst his powers were limited by an imperial diet reuniting representatives from more than 200 cities, counties, principalities, and prelatures. While some colonial empires practised mass slaughter and violent imposition, others, like the British, tried to coexist with traditional local rules (an attempt that permitted the formation of the still existing Commonwealth of Nations, with 53 members encompassing 30 percent of the world's population).

In fact, most empires in the past were organized as "mixed" regimes of self-government and authoritarianism. Some, like Japan, adapted in recent times the institutional figure of the traditional emperor to the uses of a parliamentary monarchy. This and other contemporary very large units, prominently including the USA and the EU, must be considered democratic empires.

In the long term there is an ever-continuing trend toward larger empires. There is no evidence of empires larger than 10,000 square kilometers much before 3000 BC. The largest ancient empires, in Egypt and Mesopotamia, with about one million square kilometers, were still tiny compared to the present ones. The largest ones at the beginning of our era, in China and Rome, were already much larger, with about five million square kilometers. But modern empires, including Russia and the colonial empires of Spain and Britain, have encompassed double-digit millions of square kilometers.

This continuing trend toward larger sizes of empires has been enabled, above all, by technological advances in transport and communications. In the sixteenth century Charles V, king of the Spanish empire, where "the sun never set," and emperor of the Holy Roman and German empire, is said to have spent more than one-fourth of his 40 years of tenure traveling – 3,600 days by horse and 200 by ship, having slept in 3,200 different beds. Roads, canals, harbors, railways, and highways have always formed the skeleton of empires. But things changed dramatically with the invention of the telegraph in the nineteenth century, later followed by the telephone and the internet, which created the age of instant communication. The art of government at a distance has multiplied the size of viable empires.

Another historical trend is towards an increasing number of simultaneous empires, so that the imperial form of government includes increasingly higher proportions of the world's population. Virtually none of the territories of the currently existing states in the world has been alien or outside some large modern empire. Among the very few exceptions are Thailand (which emerged from the old kingdom of Siam without Western colonization) and Israel (which was created from scratch in 1948).

The present world is organized in at least five very large, powerful empires. In alphabetical order, which may coincide with the order of their relative strength, they are: America, China, Europe, Japan, and Russia. These five political units encompass nowadays about 40 percent of the world's population (and 80 percent of the world's production). Five more very large units can also be considered of the imperial type, at least in terms of the size and variety of their population, and, in most cases, the multilevel federal style of their internal organization. They are: Indonesia, Brazil and India, closely linked to Pakistan and Bangladesh (Australia and Canada have comparable territorial sizes to the empires mentioned, but they are heavily under-populated). In all ten units together live more than two-thirds of the world's populations at the beginning of the twenty-first century, as shown in Table 1.1.

These two lists of current "empires," which are determined by population sizes, can be disputed. But in practice their composition largely coincides with the workings of some of the most influential worldwide organizations. The so-called Group of Eight (G8) aimed at gathering together the main world powers, reunited the United States of America, as well as its highly developed neighbor Canada and the four most powerful member states of the EU, that is Britain, France, Germany, and Italy, with Japan and Russia. Only China, of the top five empires listed above, is absent (but it has already participated at some meetings of the finance ministers of the G8). In the more formal Security Council of the United Nations Organization, five members enjoy veto power over collective decisions: America, China, Russia and the two European countries who won (or claim to have won) the Second World War, Britain and France. In this case the list matches the above top five very closely. Also, recent plans to enlarge the Security Council include as candidates the other empire in the first list, Japan, together with Brazil and India, prominent in the second list. The countries officially possessing nuclear weapons also match the imperial list rather closely; they include America, the two European powers Britain and France, Russia, China, India and Pakistan (together with Israel and possibly some other states not yet confirmed).

A very large empire implies that no exclusionary borders exist within its territory and, therefore, the occasions for interterritorial conflicts are lower than in a setting of numerous sovereign, mutually hostile states. The empire is an umbrella for the territories included which may prevent their mutual belligerency. External imperial borders tend also to be conflictive, especially if they neighbor other empires. But a world organized in a few empires implies a shorter total length of borders and, therefore, fewer lines of potential conflict than one organized in many sovereign states.

Regretfully, a single-government world is not foreseeable from historical developments. If the tendency toward increasingly larger sizes of empire, as measured by territory, is extrapolated, we find only a 50 percent probability of a single world empire by a date placed between 2200 and 3800 (depending on which author makes the calculation). If the extrapolation is based on the proportion of the world's population within the largest empire, that expectation should be deferred to nothing less than the year 4300.

Even the United Nations accepts, in practice, acting on very important occasions as a complement to some of the largest empires, a kind of stand in for "the rest of the world," rather than as an embryo of such worldwide single government. For the most durable of present-day conflicts, that between Israel and Palestine, the so-called "quartet" in charge is composed of the USA, the EU and the Russian Federation, in addition to the United Nations Organization, which is placed at about the same level as the former three. Similarly, for dealing with North Korean threats, another quartet of the most directly involved empires is formed, under the auspices of the United Nations, by China, Japan, Russia, and the USA.

Table 1.1 Large empires

Empire (years)	Peak period	Land area (million km²)	Population (million inhabitants)
Egypt (3000 BC–525 BC)	1450 BC–1400 BC	1	3
China: Xia/Shang (1900 BC–600 BC)	1122 BC–1050 BC	1	15
Qin/Han/Xin/Jin (255 BC–316)	100–105	6	60
Tang/Song (618–1279)	715–751	6	60
Ming (1368–1644)	1450–1513	6	150
Qing (1644–1911)	1790–1840	15	460
Mesopotamia (1850 BC–608 BC)	670 BC–655 BC	1	10
Persia: Achaemenid (580 BC–330 BC)	500 BC–480 BC	5	15
Alexander (335 BC–311 BC)	323 BC–311 BC	5	20
Sassanid (227 BC–642)	550–600	3	5
India: Magadha (600 BC–184 BC)	261 BC–230 BC	3	30
Huns: Xiongnu (230 BC–460)	176 BC–110 BC	9	<1
Rome (750 BC–476)	117–138	5	46
Byzantium (395–1479)	555–570	3	10
Turks (540–640)	557–582	6	6
Arab: Caliphate (622–945)	720–756	11	30
Germany: Carolingian (751–843)	800–814	1	10
Holy Roman (843–1806)	1200	<1	16
Mongol (1200–1398)	1294–1310	24	120
Golden Hordes (1310–1552)	1310–1350	6	<1
Inca (1250–1535)	1493–1532	2	4
Aztec (1440–1520)	1502–1520	<1	4
Austria (1278–1918)	1714–1720	1	18
Spain (1482–1975)	1780–1830	14	27
Portugal (1200–1975)	1820–1822	6	7
Ottoman (1307–1921)	1829–1885	5	30
Brazil (1822–)	1900–	9	18
Russia (1300–)	1895–1906	23	133
Britain (1600–1980)	1920–1936	36	620
France (1530–1962)	1920–1946	12	90
America (1690–)	1899–1945	10	150
Europe (1957–)	2007–	4	450

21st century largest units		Land area	Population 2006
China 1949–		9	1 318
India 1947–		3	1 125
Europe (EU) 1957–		4	490
America (US) 1787–		10	302
Indonesia 1945–		2	223
Brazil 1822–		9	190
Pakistan 1947–		1	164
Russia 1991–		17	143
Bangladesh 1971–		<1	150
Japan 1945–		<1	127
	Total	56	4 055
	World total	149	6 272

Note: For historical cases, the "peak period" corresponds to the period with the largest area; population is given for the "peak period."

2 Sovereign states

The "state" is a form of government that has achieved wide appeal in the modern world. Apparently, the current world is organized into almost 200 states. But only a relatively limited number of these political units can be considered to be successful states in a strict sense of the word. Perhaps the fact that the worldwide organization reuniting all governments is called the United Nations might after all have some significance (besides that of avoiding confusion with the unit usually known as the United States).

The state as a form of government can be defined by the following characteristics:

- *Large or middle-size, in terms of both territory and population.*
- *Fixed territory and formal boundaries.* The clear establishment and foreign recognition of the territorial limits of a state are intended as protection from external attacks, invasions, immigrants, and imports.
- *Sovereignty.* The state has supreme authority over a territory and population. It recognizes no other source of jurisdiction but itself. The state's power to make ultimate decisions is recognized by other sovereign states.
- *Monopoly and homogenization.* The state has reserved functions with exclusive jurisdiction within its territory. Whether dictatorial or democratic, it is organized with an internal hierarchy of powers. In order to facilitate the exercise of its functions and consummate its exclusiveness, it tends to establish a uniform administration over the territory, as well as to promote the homogenization of important social and cultural characteristics of its subjects or citizens.

As can be seen, these characteristics are in sharp contrast with the corresponding definition of "empire" presented above as an alternative form of political community. Actually, the first modern states emerged from and consolidated themselves against previously existing empires. In Europe, the so-called Thirty Years' War, which was triggered by the Protestant challenge against the Holy Roman and German Empire, led to decisive weakening of imperial structures. The war ended with the treaty of Westphalia in 1648, by which the imperial territory was partitioned between increasingly stronger sovereign states, above all France and Sweden. Across most of the European territory, clear borders were drawn and mutually recognized by emerging states. At the same time, the states, which were organized as absolutist monarchies, tried to absorb hundreds of traditional autonomous territories, cities, small republics, and principalities under a single centralized power, whether by military conquest, dynastic combination or even mutual agreement.

The earliest political units deserving to be called states were England, France, Spain, and Sweden, which were formed on territories located at the periphery of the former Western Roman Empire. Out of imperial control, each of the four states mentioned could organize a new, highly centralized command of its territory from a newly privileged capital city – London, Paris, Madrid, and Stockholm, respectively. During the eighteenth century all of these states combined occupied only between two or three percent of the earth's territory, while all other parts of the world were organized in small political units and larger empires of various formulas. New large states were also formed later in the core territory of the Roman Empire – Germany, and Italy –, but in these cases in a much more decentralized way based on the aggregation of networks of middle-sized cities and regions.

The largest modern states tended to organize heavy military apparatuses and fought frequent and highly lethal wars. The states created professional diplomacy and espionage, as well as the authority to require, give, deny or retire passports. Against the medieval universality of the Christian church, state rulers determined the religion of their subjects and appointed bishops and abbots. Each modern state tried to excel in providing internal standardization of weights and measures, a common currency within its territory, and civil law, by these means helping to consolidate relatively large markets.

Typically, each state attempted to create a culturally unified "nation" by means of repression, coercion, symbols and compulsory school. But very few European states had any obvious ethnic or linguistic unity and not all were equally successful at integrating disparate local units. A centralized control of the territory was instrumental in establishing external borders and affirming sovereignty in the face of other states. Certain newly peripheralized regions, given the increasing costs of secession, acquiesced to integration, but developed innovative demands for participation and power sharing within the state, thus challenging the homogenizing design.

Elsewhere, the European model of the sovereign state has been much less successful. The United States of America was created from the beginning as a "compound republic" (rather than as a nation–state) formed by previously existing units retaining their constituent powers. Instead of concentrating power around a single center as in the European-style states, the American empire is organized with a "checks and balances" regime based on division of powers, negotiations and jurisprudence. In Asia, a few very large, over-populated empires have also escaped from the project of "statization:" China, the combined India–Pakistan–Bangladesh, Indonesia, and Japan have maintained certain traditional imperial characteristics of internal complexity, not adopting the homogenizing features of modern European states mentioned above.

Unlike in either North America or Asia, attempts to replicate the typical European "state" form of government were made in Hispanic America, Africa, and the Middle East as a consequence of the colonial expansion of European states and the further independence of their colonies. Indeed, the larger and more powerful states of Europe, which had been created as an alternative formula to empires, engendered new colonial empires in other parts of the world. When the people of the colonies rid themselves of imperial domination, the European states turned inward to create a new common empire in Europe – as will be analyzed in another part of this book. But still more paradoxically, the former colonies, in gaining independence, also lost the large-scale networks of imperial size and did nothing but imitate the old "state" forms of government of their former masters. The experience has been much less successful than it was in the metropolis – in many cases, indeed, a failure.

Since the foundation period of states in Europe, four waves of "statization" of the world can be distinguished, each of them punctuated by major wars and the dissolution of large empires, as detailed in Table 2.1, at the end of this chapter. At the time of the congress of the greater powers in Vienna in 1815, there were barely one dozen states in Europe, together with numerous traditional small political units. The first wave of formation of states started with the dissolution of the Spanish empire in the Americas, greatly aided by the destructive effects of the Napoleonic wars in Europe. The Spanish colonies split from the empire and almost immediately split up themselves after some new Pan-American projects failed. The four large Spanish colonial viceroyalties had become 15 republics of disparate size and composition by 1840. But most of the new republics had to be improvised under conditions of precarious colonial legacy, internal ethnic dispersion, and isolation from other world markets. They emerged as very weak states, in the sense that they attained only ineffective armies, tiny administrative structures, and little law enforcement. Some of them did not achieve even minimal degrees of institutionalization and social and political stability in the ensuing two hundred years.

The second wave of state formation arose during the First World War and with the fall of the Austro-Hungarian, Ottoman and Russian empires. The so-called "principle of nationalities" supported by the US president Woodrow Wilson, which sought the formation of ethnically homogeneous units, had driven the creation of ten new states in Europe by 1920. However, most of the new states proved to be highly unstable and vulnerable. The aggression wars of Nazi Germany led to temporary absorption of most of them into the so-called Third German Empire, which preceded many of them becoming satellites of or being directly absorbed by the new Soviet version of the Russian empire.

The third wave of states formed after the Second World War out of the dismantling of the European colonial empires, especially the British and the French (but also the Belgian, Dutch, German, Portuguese, and Spanish) in Southeast Asia, Africa and the Middle East. Not less than 40 new independent states were created between 1945 and 1960, and about 30 more by 1975. The number of states in the world was thus more than doubled within a period of 30 years. Particularly in Africa and the Middle East, many of the new political units were organized within borders that had been capriciously drawn as straight lines, like a painting by Mondrian, by the former colonialists. These frequently contained high ethnic heterogeneity. Pan-African projects such as the "Negritude" rapidly dissolved. Also, the Arab League did not become a solid institutional network but only a setting for occasional relations among sultans and military dictators. In certain parts of Asia, a continent that, as mentioned, had remained mostly dominated by very old empires, the British colonization had been relatively more respectful of previous territorial structures since it had been organized by means of private companies and indirect rule through local chiefs.

However, in general, many of the new independent African, Southeast Asian and Middle Eastern rulers were capable of neither maintaining internal order nor controlling their borders or defending the territory from foreign attacks. Governments made scarce distinction between private and public spheres and promoted rulers' business and even private armies, while ineffective, corrupt and irrelevant bureaucracies caused many people to remain attached to their own networks and local institutions. Violent conflicts, civil wars and secession attempts proliferated. In many cases, the very idea of "state" was frustrated since the new political units achieved neither internal monopoly nor external sovereignty.

The fourth wave of states developed as a consequence of the end of the Cold War, which brought about the Soviet disunion of the Russian empire and the disintegration of the multiethnic Yugoslavia. Within a couple of years after 1991, 20 new independent republics were created in Central and Eastern Europe and Central Asia. Eventually, many of these either sought their salvation by applying for membership of the increasingly large, democratic and market oriented European empire, or languished, isolated, in the hands of dictatorial and ineffectual rulers. In particular, the new three Baltic republics, Estonia, Latvia, and Lithuania, as an example of the most fortunate of cases, passed almost directly from the Soviet Union to the European Union. But others, such as Georgia and Ukraine, were left at the doors, which affected their internal stability.

Aside from the ten very large empires mentioned above, it could be said that the better established "states" are the few units that have been accepted as members of the Organization of Economic Cooperation and

Development, since, according to the organization's criteria, they must share a commitment to democratic government, good governance, and a market economy. In total, including those within the largest empires, they are 30 states, of which 23 are in Europe (including 19 members of the EU), three in North America (each of imperial dimensions), two in Asia, and two in Oceania.

Elsewhere, the chances of establishing middle-sized or large sovereign and effective states are highly improbable. Actually, the higher the number of attempts to build new states, the weaker seem to have been the subsequent results. An effective state, indeed, requires an extremely costly initial accumulation of resources into the hands of the public authority, a condition detrimental to the opportunities for private initiatives, at least at some foundation stage. Building a new public administration able to impose order, guard the borders and collect taxes over a large territory requires heavy, labor-intensive investments, which may imply net losses for the economic activity of the subjects. Only when the size of the bureaucracy is sufficiently large can it be more technologically intensive and produce outputs with net social benefits.

The larger European states achieved efficiency through long, violent and very cruel processes of internal and external war-making and concentration of power at the expense of their subjects. But many countries have not reached this stage of statehood development. New, smaller states splitting from robust states may have an advantage because they can rely upon previously existing structures and mechanisms. But former colonies or other deprived territories without administrative resources may be unable to achieve minimum levels of state effectiveness.

In several dozen countries at the bottom of the scale of statehood, government has actually ceased to function, if ever it did. This means that the central rulers have no control over most of the state's territory; they are very ineffective in collecting taxes; they do not provide even the most basic goods and services (not even money coinage, for instance); there are epidemic diseases, widespread crime, disorder, conflict, and rebellions; natural disasters become highly destructive; and people massively emigrate up to the point that emigrants' remittances become the first source of income for natives (however, these states typically display splendid presidential palaces and colorful flags and postage stamps).

There are several accounts of failed states in the current world. The World Bank holds a permanently revised list of "fragile states," called LICUS (for "low income countries under stress"), to be given priority, but in most cases impotent, foreign aid. There are between 30 and 40 of these countries, including "collapsed or failing states," others in permanent internal conflict, several with large territories and populations (like the Democratic Republic of the Congo, Myanmar, Nigeria, Sudan, Uzbekistan), as well as other small isolated unviable nations, encompassing all together between five and ten percent of the world's population. In another comparable report,

Britain's Department for International Development has named 46 "fragile states" of concern.

An extreme example of a failed state is Somalia, located in the Horn of Africa, which has been formally independent since 1960 and at intermittent civil war since the mid-1970s. Somalia has no effective central government authority, no national currency nor any other feature associated with a well-established state. De facto authority is in the hands of the unrecognized entities of Somaliland, Puntland and other small groups of rival warlords and Muslim guerrillas. About 20 countries in Central and West Africa (out of 51 African countries) and about ten more in Asia and the former Soviet Union are usually described as having similar features. Comparable conditions can also be observed in about a dozen countries in Central America, the Andean region and the Caribbean Sea.

Table 2.1 The formation of current states

Europe	America	Africa	Asia–Pacific
San Marino 301–	US America 1787–		China 1900 BC–
Denmark 980–	Haiti 1804–		Japan 660 BC–
France 987–			Persia → Iran 580 BC–
England → UK 1066–			Vietnam 938–1893 →
Andorra 1278–			Myanmar→Burma 1057–1885→
Monaco 1297–			Ottoman → Turkey 1307–
Spain 1492–			Oman 1741–
Switzerland 1499–			Afghanistan 1746–1888 →
Sweden 1521–			Siam → Thailand 1767–
Russia → USSR → Russia 1547–			Nepal 1769–
Netherlands 1568–			
Portugal 1139, 1640–			
Liechtenstein 1806–			

First wave 1815–1910

Europe	America	Africa	Asia–Pacific
Greece 1827–	Argentina 1816–	Egypt 1827–1855 →	Australia 1901–
Belgium 1830–	Paraguay 1816–	Liberia 1847–	New Zealand 1907–
Luxembourg 1867–	Chile 1818–	Ethiopia 1855–	
Montenegro 1868–1915→	Colombia 1821–	South Africa 1910–	
Italy 1870–	Mexico 1821–		
Germany 1871–	Venezuela 1829–		
Serbia 1878–1915 →	Brazil 1822–		
Bulgaria 1878–	Costa Rica 1840–		
Rumania 1878–	El Salvador 1840–		
Norway 1905–	Guatemala 1840–		
	Honduras 1840–		
	Nicaragua 1840–		
	Peru 1824–		
	Bolivia 1825–		
	Ecuador 1830–		
	Uruguay 1830–		
	Dominican R. 1844–		
	Canada 1867–		
	Cuba 1902–		
	Panama 1903–		

Second wave 1913–1944

Albania 1913–
Finland 1917–
Austria R. 1918–
Estonia 1918–1940 →
Hungary 1918–
Latvia 1918–1940 →
Lithuania 1918–1940 →
Poland 1918–
→Yugoslavia 1918–2000 →
Czechoslovakia 1919–1992 →
Ireland 1921–
Vatican 1929–
Iceland 1944–

→ Egypt 1922–

Yemen 1918–
→ Afghanistan 1919–
Mongolia 1921–
Iraq 1932–
Saudi Arabia 1932–

Third wave 1945–1986

Cyprus 1960–
Malta 1964–

Jamaica 1962–
Trinidad–Tobago 1962–
Barbados 1966–
Guyana 1966–
Bahamas 1973–
Grenada 1974–
Surinam 1975–
Dominica 1978–
Sainte Lucia 1979–
St. Vincent–Gren. 1979–
Antigua–Barbuda 1981–
Belize 1981–
Saint Kitts–Nevis 1983–

Libya 1951–
Morocco 1956–
Sudan 1956–
Tunisia 1956–
Ghana 1957–
Guinea 1958–
Benin 1960–
Burkina Faso 1960–
Cameroon 1960–
Central African R. 1960–
Chad 1960–
Congo 1960–
Congo D.R. 1960–
Cote d'Ivoire 1960–

Korea 1945–
Indonesia 1945–
Syria 1945–
Jordan 1946–
Lebanon 1946–
Philippines 1946–
India 1947–
Pakistan 1947–
→Burma→Myanmar 1948–
Israel 1948–
Korea P.R. 1948–
Sri Lanka 1948–
Bhutan 1949–
Taiwan 1949–

Continued

Table 2.1—cont'd

Europe	America	Africa	Asia–Pacific
		Gabon 1960–	Cambodia 1953–
		Madagascar 1960–	Laos 1954–
		Mali 1960–	→ Vietnam 1954–
		Mauritania 1960–	Malaysia 1957–
		Niger 1960–	Kuwait 1961–
		Nigeria 1960–	Samoa 1962–
		Senegal 1960–	Maldives 1965–
		Sierra Leone 1960–	Singapore 1965–
		Somalia 1960–	Nauru 1968–
		Togo 1960–	Fiji 1970–
		Algeria 1962–	Tonga 1970–
		Burundi 1962–	Bahrain 1971–
		Rwanda 1962–	Bangladesh 1971–
		Uganda 1962–	Qatar 1971–
		Kenya 1963–	United Arab Emirates 1971–
		Tanzania 1964–	Papua–New Guinea 1975–
		Zambia 1964–	Solomon 1978–
		Malawi 1964–	Tuvalu 1978–
		Gambia 1965–	Kiribati 1979–
		Rhodesia → Zimbabwe1965–	Vanuatu 1980–
		Botswana 1966–	Brunei 1984–
		Lesotho 1966–	Marshall 1986–
		Equatorial Guinea 1968–	Micronesia 1986–
		Mauritius 1968–	
		Swaziland 1968–	
		Cape Verde 1974–	
		Guinea–Bissau 1974–	
		Angola 1975–	
		Comoros 1975–	
		Mozambique 1975–	
		Sao Tome–Principe 1975–	
		Seychelles 1976–	
		Djibouti 1977–	

Fourth wave 1990–

Namibia 1990–
Eritrea 1993–

Kazakhstan 1991–
Kyrgyzstan 1991–
Tajikistan 1991–
Turkmenistan 1991–
Uzbekistan 1991–
Palau 1994–
Timor East 2002–

Armenia 1991–
Azerbaijan 1991–
Belarus 1991–
Croatia 1991–
→Estonia 1991–
Georgia 1991–
→ Latvia 1991–
→ Lithuania 1991–
Macedonia 1991–
Moldova 1991–
Slovenia 1991–
Ukraine 1991–
Bosnia–Herzegovina 1992–
→ Czech R. 1992–
Slovakia 1992–
→ Serbia 2000–
→ Montenegro 2006–

3 Small nations

There have always been hundreds or thousands of small political units with high levels of autonomy or independence, typically within large empires. Before the formation of states within Europe developed out of the Westphalia treaty in the seventeenth century, the Roman and German empire encompassed about 300 autonomous territories, including among the largest Bavaria, Saxony, and Brandenburg–Prussia, together with the tiny territories of Baden, Hesse, Cologne, and Salzburg. In Swiss territory, both small rural cantons and cities, like Geneva and Berne, governed themselves. On the Italian peninsula, the kingdom of Naples and the Papal dominions coexisted with tiny principalities like Parma and robust city-republics like Florence, Genoa and Venice. Other well-governed small or middle-sized kingdoms and principalities existed in Bohemia, Brittany, Catalonia, Scotland, and Sicily, among other places. On the basis of these and many other similar experiences, medieval assemblies summoned by the kings were formed with representatives not only of diverse social categories but also of well-defined small territories. Even the largest kingdoms, like England and France, somehow relied upon county and borough elections, town assemblies, and provincial estates.

The typical medieval city, commune, canton, county, rural town, or village was formed from private associations of households organized to provide public goods such as the maintenance of a food supply, administration of justice, and military defense. Eventually they ignored the primacy of the emperor or the Pope, began to rule on their own and coalesced with similar units to form republics and principalities. Likewise, the British colonies in North America were, before declaring independence and forming a large confederation, small business agrarian corporations and public good providers that were able to govern themselves on most issues, since their members clearly shared some basic common interests. The Spanish colonies in North and South America were also partly organized on the basis of small municipalities, parishes, and towns, together with surviving American Indian republics.

The dissolution of large empires, the formation of new sovereign states with centralized administrative structures and the independence of the colonies dramatically changed the forms of territorial organization across the world. However, the survival and resilience of traditional small political units, as well as the ever-continuing human tendency to form small-scale units of conviviality and collective decision making, seems irrepressible. After all, a political community is nothing other than a group of individuals who accept that collective decisions made within their ambit will be binding and enforceable. This acceptance and mutual commitment can, of course, be facilitated by a high degree of economic and cultural homogeneity among members as well as by the existence of clearly identifiable common interests. In contrast, in large, heterogeneous or deeply divided communities, there is likely to be a group of absolute winners, whose endurance may induce the losers either to resist the enforcement of collective decisions, not comply with them, rebel, secede, or emigrate.

More than two thirds of the world's population lives nowadays either in small countries or under the jurisdiction of small non-state governments with legislative powers. In particular, more than three-fifths of the currently recognized "states" are in fact non-sovereign small political units. About 70 of these units are mini-countries with a population of between one and ten million inhabitants (including, for example, Botswana, Estonia, Ireland, Singapore and Uruguay) and 40 more are micro-countries with less than one million inhabitants (for instance: Andorra, Barbados, Comoros, Maldives and Vanuatu). Small, formally independent states have proliferated alongside the expansion of military alliances and transnational markets, permitting those "states" to save some of the basic public goods that had defined the sovereignty of the first modern large states, including a costly army and a single currency. Precisely because they do not have to pay the heavy burdens of classical statehood, small countries in an open international environment can benefit from their internal homogeneity and inclination to democracy.

In addition, there are more than 500 non-state political units with governments and legislative powers located within a couple of dozen decentralized empires or large federal states (with outstanding cases including the Basque country, Bavaria, Catalonia, Flanders, Kashmir, Quebec, and Scotland). There are also about 20 "territories" formally linked but physically non-contiguous to some large empire or state and in fact quite independent (such as Bermuda, Greenland, and Puerto Rico), and about 15 other territories de facto seceded from recognized states (most notoriously Palestine and Taiwan). About 150 of these non-state small units are in Europe, nearly 200 in the Americas, about 150 in Asia and about 40 in Africa, as listed in Table 3.1, at the end of the chapter.

The "imperial" nature (in the sense presented in this book) of some of the very large federations encompassing numerous small political units seems to be implicitly reflected in the fact that many of the latter are officially called "states," like those within the United States of America, Australia, Austria, Brazil, India, Malaysia, Mexico, or Venezuela, or even "free states" in some cases in Germany, "republics" as in Russia, or "nations" in the United Kingdom, together with other names like "cantons," "provinces," "regions," "territories," or "autonomous communities" in other parts of the world.

Most of all these small political units with high degrees of autonomy share the following defining characteristics:

- *small size* in terms of both territory and population
- *high degrees of ethnic homogeneity* as defined for the racial, language and religious characteristics of their members (see References at the end of this book for details.)
- *simple and soft forms of government* based on the ease with which they form a social majority supporting collective, enforceable decisions.

In some imperial areas, and in particular within the European Union, the difference between formal independence and autonomy is a question of degree. Not even the larger states are nowadays effectively sovereign, since they have ceded most of their decision making powers in monetary and economic policy, defense and military affairs, and legislation in other fields to the Union (or to other intergovernmental agreements and alliances in other parts of the world). Large states with federal structures have no internal power monopoly either. At the imperial, the state and the local levels, rather than sovereignty and monopoly, sharing power becomes a general norm.

Regarding small political units, for most of them, two variables can explain where they stand: the relative size of the unit and its degree of internal homogeneity. These two variables are crucially related to the workability of democratic forms of government. If the small unit is sufficiently large within a large state, it can expect to be influential in statewide decisions and it is thus likely to be ready to accept the decisions made by democratic means at the level of the state. If the small unit is sufficiently homogeneous, it will also be able to develop a socially satisfactory democratic self-government. On the contrary, a too-small unit within a large state will tend to feel alienated from statewide collective decisions and seek secession if this is viable. But if the small unit is ethnically heterogeneous, it may also face difficulties in governing itself.

Table 3.1 Nations of the world

Europe	America	Africa	Asia–Pacific
Austria *Lands*: Burgenland, Carinthia, Lower Austria, Upper Austria, Salzburg, Styria Steiermark, Tyrol, Vorarlberg, Vienna.	**U.S. America** *States*: Alabama, Alaska, Arizona, Arkansas, California, Colorado, Connecticut, Delaware, Florida, Georgia, Hawaii, Idaho, Illinois, Indiana, Iowa, Kansas, Kentucky, Louisiana, Maine, Maryland, Massachusetts, Michigan, Minnesota, Mississippi, Missouri, Montana, Nebraska, Nevada, New Hampshire, New Jersey, New Mexico, New York, North Carolina, North Dakota, Ohio, Oklahoma, Oregon, Pennsylvania, Rhode Island, South Carolina, South Dakota, Tennessee, Texas, Utah, Vermont, Virginia, Washington, West Virginia, Wisconsin, Wyoming. *Capital*: District of Columbia. *Commonwealths*: Northern Mariana I., Puerto Rico. *Territories*: American Samoa, Guam, Virgin I.	**Morocco** *Seceded*: Western Sahara.	**China** *Provinces*: Anhui, Fujian, Gansu, Guangdong, Guizhou, Hainan, Hebei, Heilongjiang, Henan, Hubei, Hunan, Jiangsu, Jiangxi, Jilin, Liaoning, Qinghai, Shaanxi, Shandong, Shanxi, Sichuan, Yunnan, Zhejiang. *Autonomous Regions*: Guangxi Zhuang, Inner Mongolia, Ningxia Hui, Xinjiang Uighur (East Turkistan), Tibet. *Special regions*: Hong Kong, Macau. *Seceded*: Taiwan.
Belgium *Regions*: Brussels, Flanders, Wallonia.		**Nigeria** *States*: Abia, Adamawa, Akwa Ibom, Anambra, Bauchi, Bayelsa, Benue, Borno, Cross River, Delta, Ebonyi, Edo, Ekiti, Enugu, Gombe, Imo, Jigawa, Kaduna, Kano, Katsina, Kebbi, Kogi, Kwara, Lagos, Nassarawa, Niger, Ogun, Ondo, Osun, Oyo, Plateau, Rivers, Sokoto, Taraba, Yobe, Zamfara. *Federal Capital Territory*: Abuja.	**Comoros** *Seceded*: Anjouan, Moheli.
Britain *Nations*: Northern Ireland, Scotland, Wales. *Bailiwicks*: Jersey, Guernsey (Channel I.). *Overseas territories*: Anguilla, Bermuda, British Virgin I., Cayman I., Gibraltar, Montserrat, Turks and Caicos I.		**Somalia** *Seceded*: Somaliland.	**India** *States*: Andhra Pradesh, Arunachal Pradesh, Assam, Bihar, Chhattisgarh, Goa, Gujarat, Haryana, Himachal Pradesh, Jammu and Kashmir, Jharkhand, Karnataka, Kerala, Madhya Pradesh, Maharashtra, Manipur, Meghalaya, Mizoram, Nagaland, Orissa, Punjab, Rajasthan, Sikkim,
Denmark *Autonomous region*: Faroe I. *Self-governing division*: Greenland.		**South Africa** *Provinces*: Eastern Cape, Free State, Gauteng, KwaZulu-Natal, Mpumalanga, Limpopo, Northern Cape, North West, Western Cape.	
Finland *Autonomous government*: Åland.	**Canada** *Provinces*: Alberta, British Columbia, Manitoba, New Brunswick, Newfoundland,	**Tanzania** *State*: Zanzibar.	
France *Special region*: Corse.			

Continued

Table 3.1—cont'd

Europe	America	Africa	Asia–Pacific
Non-legislative regions: Alsace, Aquitaine, Auvergne, Basse-Normandie, Bourgogne, Bretagne, Centre, Champagne–Ardenne, Franche-Comté, Haute-Normandie, Île-de-France, Languedoc-Roussillon, Limousin, Lorraine, Midi-Pyrénées, Nord-Pas-de-Calais, Pays de la Loire, Picardie, Poitou-Charentes Provence-Alpes-Cote d'Azur, Rhône-Alpes.	Nova Scotia, Ontario, Prince Edward, Quebec, Saskatchewan.		Tamil Nadu, Tripura, Uttaranchal, Uttar Pradesh, West Bengal. *Territories:* Andaman and Nicobar Islands, Chandigarh, Dadra and Nagar Haveli, Daman and Diu, Lakshadweep, Pondicherry. *Capital territory:* Delhi.
Overseas: *Departments:* Guadeloupe, Martinique, French Guiana, Reunion. *Collectivities:* Mayotte, New Caledonia; *Country:* Polynesia.	**Argentina** *Provinces:* Buenos Aires, Catamarca, Chaco, Chubut, Córdoba, Corrientes, Entre Ríos, Formosa, Jujuy, La Pampa, La Rioja, Mendoza, Misiones, Neuquén, Río Negro, Salta, San Juan, San Luis, Santa Cruz, Santa Fe, Santiago del Estero, Tierra del Fuego Antarctica and South Atlantic Islands, Tucumán. *Federal district:* Buenos Aires.		**Indonesia** *Provinces:* Western New Guinea: West Irian Jaya, West Papua. Java: Banten, Central Java, East Java, West Java. Kalimantan (in Borneo): Central Kalimantan, East Kalimantan, South Kalimantan, West Kalimantan. Maluku Islands: Maluku, North Maluku. Bali and Nusa Tenggara: Bali, East Nusa Tenggara, West Nusa Tenggara. Sulawesi: Central Sulawesi, Gorontalo, North Sulawesi, South East Sulawesi, South Sulawesi, West Sulawesi. Sumatra: Bangka-Belitung, Bengkulu, Jambi, Lampung, North Sumatra, Riau, Riau Islands, South Sumatra, West Sumatra. *Special regions:* Aceh, Yogyakarta. *Capital city district:* Jakarta.
Germany *Lands:* Baden-Württemberg, Bavaria, Berlin (city), Brandenburg, Bremen (city), Hamburg (city), Hesse, Mecklenburg–West Pomerania, Lower Saxony, Northern Rhine–Westphalia, Rhineland–Palatinate, Saarland, Saxony, Saxony-Anhalt, Schleswig-Holstein, Thuringia.	**Bolivia** *Departments:* Beni, Chuquisaca, Cochabamba, La Paz, Oruro, Pando, Potosí, Santa Cruz, Tarija.		
Italy *Regions:* Abruzzo, Aosta, Abulia, Basilicata, Calabria, Campania, Emilia-Romagna, Friuli-Venezia	**Brazil** *States:* Acre, Halagaos, Amapá, Amazonas, Bahia, Ceará, Espírito Santo, Goiás, Maranhão, Mato Grosso, Mato Grosso do Sul, Minas Gerais, Pará, Paraíba, Paraná, Rio Grande do Sul, Rondônia,		

Giulia, Latium, Liguria, Lombardy, Marches, Molise, Piedmont, Sardinia, Sicily, Trentino–South Tyrol, Tuscany, Umbria, Veneto.

Netherlands
Autonomous countries: Aruba, New Antilles.

Portugal
Regions: North, Center, Lisbon-Valley of Tejo, Alentejo, Algarve.
Autonomous regions: Açores, Madeira.

Spain
Autonomous communities: Andalusia, Aragon, Asturias, Balearic, Basque, Canary, Cantabria, Catalonia, Castile–La Mancha, Castile–Leon, Extremadura, Galicia, La Rioja, Madrid, Murcia, Navarre, Valencia.
Autonomous cities: Ceuta, Melilla.

Switzerland
Cantons:
Aargau, Appenzel Ausserrhoden, Appenzel Innerrhoden, Basel–Landschaft, Basel–Stadt, Bern, Freeburg, Geneva, Glarus, Graubünden, Jura, Lucerne, Neuchâtel, Nidwalden, Obwalden, Schaffhausen, Schwyz, Solothurn, St Gallen, Thurgau, Ticino, Uri, Valais, Vaud, Zug, Zurich.

Roraima, Santa Catarina, São Paulo Sergipe, Tocantins.

Mexico
States: Aguascalientes, Baja California, Baja California Sur, Campeche, Chiapas, Chihuahua, Coahuila, Colima, Durango, Guanajuato, Guerrero, Hidalgo, Jalisco, Mexico, Michoacán, Morelos, Nayarit, Nuevo León, Oaxaca, Puebla, Querétaro, Quintana Roo, San Luis Potosí, Sinaloa, Sonora, Tabasco, Tamaulipas, Tlaxcala, Veracruz, Yucatán, Zacatecas.
Federal district: Mexico City.

Venezuela
States: Amazonas, Anzoátegui, Apure, Aragua, Barinas, Bolívar, Carabobo, Cojedes, Delta Amacuro, Falcón, Guárico, Lara, Mérida, Miranda, Monagas, Nueva Esparta, Portuguesa, Sucre, Táchira, Trujillo, Vargas, Yaracuy, Zulia.
Capital district: Caracas.

Iraq
Autonomous region: Kurdistan.

Jordan
National Authority: Palestine.

Malaysia
States: Johor, Kedah, Kelantan, Kuala Lumpur, Malacca, Negeri, Sembilan, Pahang, Perak, Perlis, Penang, Wilayah Persekutuan, Selangor, Terengganu.
Territories (in Borneo): Labuan, Sabah, Sarawak.

Myanmar
Seceded: Karen, Shan.

Pakistan
Seceding: Kashmir.

Sri Lanka
Seceded: Tamil Eelam.

Turkey
Seceded: Northern Cyprus.

United Arab Emirates
Emirates: Abu Dhabi, Ajman, Al Fujayrah, Sharjah, Dubai, Ra's al Khaymah, Umm al Qaywayn.

Uzbekistan
Autonomous republic: Karakalpak.

Continued

Table 3.1—cont'd

Europe	America	Africa	Asia–Pacific
Bosnia–Herzegovina *Republics*: Bosniak/Croat Federation of Bosnia and Herzegovina, Bosnian Serb Republika Srpska. **Serbia** *States*: Serbia, Kosovo. **Russia** *Republics*: Adygeva, Altai, Bashkortostan, Buryatia, Chuvashia, Dagestan, Ingushetia, Kabardino–Balkaria, Kalmykia, Karachay–Cherkessia, Karelia, Khakassia, Komi, Mari El, Mordovia, North Ossetia–Alania, Sakha, Tatarstan, Tuva, Udmurtia. *Seceded*: Chechnya. **Azerbaijan** *Autonomous republic*: Nakhichevan. *Seceded*: Nagorno-Karabakh. **Georgia** *Autonomous region*: Ajaria. *Seceded*: Abkhazia, South Ossetia. **Moldova** *Autonomous region*: Gagauzia. *Seceded*: Transnistria. **Ukraine** *Autonomous republic*: Crimea.			**Australia** *States*: New South Wales, Victoria, Queensland, South Australia, Western Australia, Tasmania. *Capital territory*: Canberra. *Territory*: Northern Darwin. **New Zealand** *Free associate states*: Cook Islands, Niue. **Papua New Guinea** *Seceding*: Bougainville.

4   Nation building and deconstructing

The 200 or so members of the United Nations can be differentiated within a few categories, according to the definitions and discussion given in the previous chapters. There are, in the current world, about ten very large empires containing several hundred small units with legislative assemblies and executive governments. There are also about three dozen successful large states. The larger ones tend to be organized with federal formulas containing smaller political units. A similar number of states can be considered to have failed. And we can count more than 100 small nations (including most members of the EU) that would hardly be viable as independent countries without large networks of "imperial" size.

More detailed analyses of historical developments and future forecasts for specific political units can be developed on the basis of the two variables mentioned in the previous chapter: the unit's relative size and internal homogeneity. We can distinguish:

- *Empire* which can be either internally homogeneous or varied, but usually without significant ethnic or territorial confrontation between differentiated groups.
- *State* which can be either a "nation–state," where a majority group assimilates the others, or a "multination–state," where together with the largest group, at least another smaller group is relatively large and homogeneous.
- *Nation* which may be either successful if formed by a small, homogeneous group seceding from a large state or in conflict, which is more likely to occur in internally heterogeneous groups.

This typology will be illustrated here with only a number of relevant cases, but it could be used for more systematic analysis, historical revisions and predictions about the viability of certain forms of government in different contexts.

Empire

- **Homogeneous**   There are very few cases of very large, apparently ethnically homogeneous empires with no distinguishable small groups. In modern times, Japan seems to be the best case.
- **Varied**   Much more frequently, an empire includes many different small groups. If they are distributed in a way that makes no group able to rule over the others, federal arrangements can be accepted and remain stable.

A prominent case of an ethnically varied, federal empire in present times is, of course, the United States of America, whose population has different migrant origins and varied backgrounds, as well as high levels of internal mobility across the territory (although Puerto Rico is still now a disputed territory). In China the appearance of some high degree of homogeneity may be only the perception of the ignorant external observer, since important economic, language and religious differences exist among its inhabitants (also, Taiwan works in practice as an independent state and seceding movements are active in Hong Kong and Tibet). Other large federal empires with moderate internal variety are Brazil, India, and Indonesia (the latter two cases are also experiencing territorial conflicts around their borders, as will be commented on below).

State

- **Nation–state**   In the typical situation, there is a majority, homogeneous group initially facing a number of small, internally heterogeneous groups that are in time annihilated by and assimilated into the patterns of the largest group. Then a large centralized state is viable and may be relatively efficient for a while, as has been discussed above.

The most prominent case is, of course, France (where, however, on the island of Corsica and in the remote former colonies of New Caledonia and Polynesia some seceding movements exist). Great Britain has also been very successful, although it has lower degrees of internal homogeneity; most of Ireland seceded and England, Scotland and Wales are actually recognized as different nations.

- **Multination–state**   Typically, there is a majority or large group that may not be strongly homogeneous, while a second or further group is sufficiently large and homogeneous to try to rule or at least influence the ruling of the state. Some internal rivalry may develop, which may lead to the establishment of a multinational state oscillating between power sharing and decentralization.

This has traditionally been the situation in Spain, where Catalonia encompasses about one-sixth of the total population as opposed to a blurred, inconclusive Castilian predominance across several differentiated regions. A comparable situation can be found in French-speaking

Quebec, which encompasses one-fourth of Canada's total population, with an English-speaking majority unevenly distributed across a vast territory. A successful case of a minority group in the past was the leadership of peripheral Piedmont in building a large Italian state; however, even in this case the Piedmontese have traditionally felt somewhat frustrated by the "incompleteness" of the unity of Italy; as an alternative, increasing regionalization of the Italian state has been promoted in recent times by the northern regions of Friuli, Lombardy, Piedmont and Venice.

A more unstable and potentially conflictive variant exists when there are only two homogeneous groups of similar size within a state. In this situation, each group can expect to be able to form a political majority and rule over the other, or share power in an advantageous position, which may foster rivalry for domination.

This is the case in Belgium, where a traditional French-speaking Walloon majority was replaced with a new Dutch-speaking Flemish majority in recent times, thus modifying each group's expectations and relative positions as ruler and challenger for a while. A similar situation was behind the separation of the Czech Republic and Slovakia, which produced a great deal of surprise more for its sudden occurrence than for the neatness of the cleavage.

If separation is postponed too long, however, it can make the internally divided state fall apart. This tends to be the case, for instance, in land-locked Bolivia, which is deeply divided between the western high plateau (formerly a part of the Spanish Viceroy of Peru), populated by an indigenous majority speaking Aymara and Quechua, and the eastern part (formerly of the Viceroy of La Plata, today's Argentina), with the majority being of Spanish language and origin. Similar situations exist in Peru, also divided between an Aymara and Quechua majority in the Andean highlands and a Spanish population along the coast; in Ecuador, fragmented between "mestizos" (mixed) and indigenous; and in Guatemala, divided between "ladinos" ("mestizos" and Hispanicized Indians) and indigenous Mayas.

Nation

- **Successful** A small, homogeneous group resists being crushed by a majority group within a large state. A likely option is secession and the formation of a small, internally homogeneous independent state.

  The "principle of nationalities" that was brandished at the end of the First World War was aimed at producing this type of outcome, which induced in particular the separation of Hungary and other small nations from Austria and the restoration of Poland, as well as the separation of Ireland from Great Britain. The separation of India from the British Empire also gave way to the political separation of the mostly Muslim Pakistan, which was later followed by the separation of the already territorially separated Bangladesh from Western Pakistan. But all these were still imperial-sized units and conflicts then exploded within traditional nations that found themselves split between India and Pakistan, especially Kashmir and the Punjab. The creation of the state of Israel also initiated the long fight of Palestine for its independence.

Eventually, more than a dozen small and internally rather homogeneous republics attained independence from the Soviet Union, the last version of the Russian empire, including, on the European side, Estonia, Latvia and Lithuania, as well as Armenia, Belarus and Ukraine. Other nations attempting further secession include Chechnya from Russia, Abkhazia and South Ossetia from Georgia, Nagorno-Karabakh from Azerbaijan, and Transnistria from Moldova. Likewise, the dissolution of Yugoslavia was precipitated by the independence of the small, homogeneous nations of Slovenia and Croatia and the internal conflicts in Kosovo. Elsewhere, seceding small nations include Northern Cyprus in Turkey, Western Sahara in Morocco, Namibia from South Africa, Eritrea from Ethiopia, Somaliland from Somalia, Aceh from Indonesia, Karen and Shan from Myanmar, Tamil Eelam from Sri Lanka, and Bougainville from Papua New Guinea.

- **In conflict**   A small group being permanently defeated by an alien majority within a large state is tempted by secession, but it is internally highly heterogeneous (typically including a sizeable minority attached to the ruling group in the state). Rather than neat secession, there may be "ethnic-cleansing" and forced emigration, leading to genocide, civil war, or sustained terrorism.

Cases include many of the former European colonies in Africa, which attained independence from empires within ethnically mixed borders constructed by the colonial administrators. More than a dozen recently independent African countries have experienced civil wars, while in 21 countries there have been further secession attempts. Especially lethal conflicts between different ethnic groups within a new state exploded in Nigeria, the most populated African country, where the northern Muslim Hausas crushed the southeastern Christian Igbos after the latter unsuccessfully proclaimed further independence as Biafra; in Sudan, the largest country by area in the continent, where the northern Arab-dominated government violently repressed the non-Arab south as they also attempted secession; in land-locked Rwanda, where the Tutsis and the Hutus successively massacred each other; and in Republic of the Congo (former Zaire, capital Brazzaville), where Katanga and three other provinces sought secession, and where again the Tutsis (with external support from Rwanda and Burundi) fought the Hutus (supported from the Democratic Republic of the Congo, capital Kinshasa) in the deadliest conflict in the world since the Second World War.

In the former Yugoslavia, ethnically driven mass slaughters also took place. The most lethal conflict exploded with the independence of

Bosnia–Herzegovina, a constructed compound of Muslims and Serbs where each group sought further split. In Western Europe, comparable situations of small, differentiated but internally heterogeneous territories have initiated violent confrontations between groups for and against independence from a large state. This is the case in Northern Ireland, which has always remained split between Irish Catholics and English and Scottish Protestants, as well as in the Basque country, enduringly divided between a bare majority of Basques and a large number of Spaniards.

Part II

Broad alliances, small governments

The current world is increasingly organized into a number of vast overlapping areas of "imperial" size, together with a rising number of self-governed small communities. The following chapters examine three fundamental imperial-sized relations: military and security alliances, commercial and economic agreements, and areas of language and communication. Also, the steady increase in the number of small political units is analyzed for its advantages for the expansion of democratic government.

Changes in the territorial scale of political units are driven by technological changes and human decisions. Relevant technical inventions include such crucial innovations, in more or less chronological order, as language, writing, the compass, printing, gunpowder, railways, the telegraph, aviation, nuclear energy, and the internet (to which aspirin and antibiotics should probably be added in a more encompassing assessment of progress and the development of humankind). These and other inventions have dramatically reduced the costs of human exchanges, transport and communications, in this way enlarging the possible territorial scope of military operations, trade, migration and information. Just as some of these technical novelties induced the formation of relatively large states as well as made them viable in the past, others are now creating larger areas of human relations (called "empires" in this book) that make traditional states too small for efficient performance.

Specifically, broad military alliances provide small nations with an international umbrella for collective security, which may make building a new army for each new political unit unnecessary. Transnational trade agreements and common currencies make small countries viable as independent units because they no longer need to be subservient to large states' protecting markets. Linguas francas permit human beings to develop broad communications while maintaining their own local languages and cultures and avoiding the costs of forced homogenization typically imposed by large nation–states.

Thus, all these imperial-sized networks create hitherto unknown opportunities for small nations to develop new forms of self-government. The aspiration to freedom and soft forms of government, technically organized as electoral democracies in modern times, seems to be rooted in the most basic human instincts for survival and self-fulfillment. Nowadays these can be satisfied to a higher level than in any past period of human history thanks to the large-scale public goods and markets provided by imperial networks. Decentralization of large states, new forms of asymmetric federalism and the independence of new political units favour the expansion of democratic forms of government. Indeed the diffusion of democracy in the current world has been closely intertwined with the multiplication of small political nations supported by broad, transnational networks of imperial size.

5   Military alliances

Modern states were largely built as military enterprises. Traditional knights and local rulers sought to develop centralized tax collection and a bureaucracy with jurisdiction over large areas in order to finance the increasing costs of warfare. Large states attained military advantage over both vast decentralized empires and small cities or principalities. However, as the size and the power of states extended, the scale and lethality of war also expanded. The "balance of power" system based on the unquestioned sovereignty of the larger states fostered almost permanent interstate conflict, which led to the massacres of World War One and World War Two, as well as to the worldwide terror of the Cold War.

Nowadays, the world is relatively more demilitarized than it has been for several centuries. Most "states," especially the small ones (but not only these), are not even able to control their borders or defend their territory. Military strength is now heavily concentrated into a few empires. The most prominent of them, the United States of America, is a new kind of empire, which does not pretend to conquer territories in order to rule them directly, but rather to reinforce its own security. It is mainly the USA, more than international organizations, that most forcefully tries to play a vigilant role in pacifying the current interstate conflicts in the world.

War-making states

The costs of fighting, conquering territories, defending oneself and making war dramatically increased as a consequence of certain technical inventions in the mid sixteenth century. Before that, wars and disputes were basically fought with energy derived from human and animal muscles, especially hosts of warriors and cavalry. The invention of gunpowder permitted the development of portable firearms and the formation of an armed infantry. In response, the introduction of heavier arms and machinery gave way to the creation and dominance of artillery. These processes hugely increased the size and destructiveness of armies, as well as the costs of warfare.

From the end of the sixteenth century onwards, engaging in war required a standing army made up of well-trained troops. Past ad hoc recruitments of obligatory, unpaid combatants were replaced with permanent, volunteer and professional armies. Private or semi-private warrior hosts made way for state-owned, centralized military organizations. Specifically, a standing army was formed in Spain by 1570 and in Brandenburg–Prussia between 1655 and 1660; France adopted such a model between 1640 and 1680, England in 1690, the Dutch in 1693, and Russia in 1731. Standing armies initially consisted of temporary full-time soldiers ("mercenaries"), supplemented by periodic forced conscriptions. Only the diffusion of railways permitted the introduction of the obligatory military service for adult men, a formula that was adopted by several countries by the late nineteenth century.

States obtained an internal monopoly on violence by outlawing private armies and the public display or even possession of self-defense weapons by private citizens. This subsequently permitted the state to use armed agents to confront unarmed civilians. With the new warfare technologies and regular standing armies, large states enjoyed a definite war-making advantage over both decentralized empires and small cities or principalities. The concentration of military power advanced together with an increase in the administrative, technical and financial resources of the states. The size and the power of states extended as the scale of war enlarged.

Between the seventeenth and twentieth centuries, there were successive attempts to build a system of collective security based on the so-called "balance of power" between territorially bounded, heavily armed states with mutually exclusive sovereignties. A number of rulers of the great powers excelled in the art of combining diplomacy, threatening war and war-making; the list includes Richelieu and Talleyrand in France, Castlereagh in Britain and Metternich in Austria, among others. However, the "balance of power" system based on the unquestioned sovereignty of the larger states proved to be a very fragile and unstable equilibrium among hostile forces that fostered almost permanent conflict, rather than harmony.

Successive waves of war led to a series of peace treaties by which territorial conquests were apparently settled, but time and again new interstate wars broke out. During the eighteenth century there were 68 wars (counting only those having produced at least one thousand deaths in battle per year) that killed in total about four million people. They included the Spanish Succession war between Austria and France, the Seven Years' War that pitted Britain and Prussia against France, Austria and Russia, the first Russian–Turkish war and the wars triggered by the French revolution against Austria and Britain. During the nineteenth century, the number of major wars rose to 205, producing eight million deaths. They included the so-called Napoleonic wars (that confronted France with a series of coalitions formed around Austria, Britain, Prussia and Russia), the Crimean war opposing Russia to Britain, France and the Ottoman Empire, the Franco-Prussian war and a new Russo-Turkish war.

The twentieth century established itself as the most bellicose in human history. Until 1989, there were about 237 civil and interstate wars with 115 million deaths in battle (to which a similar number of civilian deaths should be added), including: the First and the Second World Wars, fought mainly among European states; the Sino-Japanese war; and a number of local wars promoted by the Cold War between the United States and the Soviet Union or China, including the Korean and the Vietnam wars.

The path of military escalation between large modern states can also be measured in the following way. As mentioned, already in the seventeeth century several states in Europe had formed permanent armies with several hundred thousand soldiers; by the early eighteenth century, about five percent of the total populations of the larger states were mobilized as troops; by the late nineteenth century this proportion had doubled; during the First World War, it had doubled again, up to 20 percent in Britain, France, Germany, Austria–Hungary and Italy. Military expenditure rose at an even faster rate. For a few years during the First World War, Britain spent more than its annual gross domestic product (GDP) on warfare, while France, Germany and Austria–Hungary spent about 80 percent of theirs; again, during the final year of the Second World War, Germany and Japan spent about 115 percent of their annual GDP on warfare.

From the fifteenth to the eighteenth centuries a significant new inter-state conflict started every two or three years; during the nineteenth century, every one or two years; and since the Second World War, every 14 months or so. Regarding the death rates per population, during the eighteenth century there were five deaths in battle per one thousand inhabitants; during the nineteenth century, six; and during the twentieth century, 46. Territorial and border disputes between "sovereign" states were the major source of war from the time of the Westphalia treaty in 1648 to the end of the Cold War in 1989.

Demilitarized nations

The end of the Cold War closed a historical period presided over by a few rival large states, their confrontational alliances and the subsequent diffusion of conflicts and wars. In particular, the dissolution of the Soviet Union implied the cancellation of the so-called Warsaw Pact, with which the Soviets and the communist dominated regimes in Central Europe had countered the North Atlantic Treaty Organization (NATO) formed by the USA and initially a dozen of its state allies in the West. Most former member states of the Warsaw Pact then joined NATO, which became an encompassing alliance of "imperial" size. Since the early 1990s, not only Russia and the former Soviet-dominated states, but also the United States, the member states of the EU and virtually every other state in the world has reduced its military expenditures or cancelled altogether any serious defense apparatus.

The relative levels of armed personnel and military expenditure in the current world are the lowest in several centuries. In the United States, the number of troops amounts to only 0.5 percent of the total population, while China is at 0.2 percent, in contrast to the two-figure proportions reported above. Military expenditure had reached 7 percent of the GDP in the USA by the mid 1980s, but it has been reduced to half of that proportion in the early twenty-first century. And whereas in the Soviet Union military expenditure had rocketed to 16 percent of GDP at the peak of the Cold War arms race, those of the current Russia are at one-fourth of that proportion.

Currently, the largest army in human terms is indeed that of overpopulated China, with about 2.3 million people, followed by the United States with 1.5 million, while all the states of the EU together could amass perhaps a figure similar to the latter. Regarding the number of heavy weapons, the balance between these three empires is even closer (with more than 30 thousand each). However, at the present stage of the technological development of warfare, the crucial variable for measuring relative military power is military expenditure. This reflects each empire's purchasing power in the arms market and the level of sophistication of its military equipment, which is increasingly associated with the use of costly electronics, communications, and information technology.

The crucial fact is that the military expenditure of the imperial USA (by 2005) was at 47 percent of the total world military expenditure, a proportion never achieved by a single power since the times of the Roman Empire. All the states of the EU together spend about 18 percent of the world total, that is, less than 40 percent of the amount the United States spends (Britain and France count for almost half of all European military strength). The other empires have been dramatically left behind: Japan spends about five percent of the world military expenditure; China, about four percent; and Russia, that is, the remnants of the formerly over-armed Soviet empire, hardly one percent. These five empires (the USA, the EU, Japan, China and Russia) together make up some 75 percent of the total world military expenditure, while they represent only 40 percent of the total population.

As for the rest, most states of the world do not enjoy even minimally effective military equipment. In many cases, they are not even able to provide effective control of their borders and a real defense of their "sovereign" territory and population. Most states in the current world spend on defense less than one percent of their GDP, that is, a lower proportion than that which old European kingdoms spent on warfare before the invention of gunpowder more than four hundred years ago – when the tools for fighting were made of iron and stone.

This general demilitarization corresponds to a situation in which the world scene is no longer one of sovereign states trying to maintain some balance of military power. Due to technological developments in transport, communications and weaponry, state or national defense is nowadays strongly linked to international security. The most prominent security tasks include the persecution and prevention of terrorism and the formation of international peacemaking and peacekeeping missions. For this, traditional patriotic, state-owned, rival armies have become obsolete. In most democratic countries, obligatory military service has been abolished; in many places, the professional soldier is also a less admired figure than in the past.

An important political implication of all this is that the costs of secession and independence of small nations from large states have decreased enormously. In many states, an army which is incapable of making serious war, attacking a neighbor or defending the country, also could not effectively prevent the independence of part of its territory. In contrast to the main waves of the development of states reviewed above, which were basically formed at the end of major international wars and the corresponding dissolution of large empires, the independence of new political units in the current world can hardly be countered with a credible threat of military intervention.

In fact, in a number of especially conflictive cases, international military missions have recently been mounted not *against* small nations' attempts at secession, but in *support* of them. Cases include the intervention of NATO forces in favor of Kosovo's secession from the rump of Yugoslavia, as well as the United Nations sponsored international missions in favor of Namibia's independence from South Africa, and of East Timor's from Indonesia. In other cases, repression of a secessionist attempt (like that of Chechnya by the Russian army) is widely condemned at international forums.

Nowadays, small autonomous or independent nations can be viable first of all because they may save the costs of building a new army. But this may require accepting and being loyal to international alliances for collective security, which may imply accepting a "balance" of military power strongly biased in favor of the USA. Thus, there are two reasons for which small nations ridding themselves of control by traditional large states may find the "Pax Americana" a favorable context: first, under an international umbrella for collective security, a state military intervention against a nation's freedom is not likely to be accepted; second, thanks to membership of an imperial military alliance providing defense and protection, it is not necessary to build a costly new army for each new political unit.

A peacemaking empire

In the present world, military strength is heavily concentrated in the USA. The foreign affairs doctrine adopted by the USA after the Cold War and especially during the presidency of George W. Bush, most clearly since 2002, postulated that the best way to establish international peace is democratization. This implied a dramatic change in American foreign policy. Statements in favor of freedom and democracy had indeed been prominent in inaugural and other major speeches of US presidents in the past, but, especially during the Cold War with the Soviet Union, it was held time and again that those American ideals contradicted its national security interests. As a matter of fact, a series of US presidents looked ready to support any pro-American, counter-revolutionary, anti-communist ruler, whether democratic or dictatorial, as a lesser evil. As in the statement attributed to both President Franklin D. Roosevelt and his secretary of state regarding petty dictators in Nicaragua and the Dominican Republic: "He is a son of a bitch, but he is ours."

For more than fifty years, American foreign policy makers tried to shape a number of checks, balances and counterweights among more or less friendly or unfriendly authoritarian regimes with the aim of having them neutralize one another and preventing the emergence of a major threat. But, as discussed above, this approach actually fostered wars and conflicts in all parts of the world.

In particular, the realist-inspired American foreign policy – emblematically represented by secretary of state Henry Kissinger in the 1960s and 1970s – made the set of military dictatorships, sultanates and absolute monarchies established in the Middle East a hotchpotch of diversified forms of violence. For a long period, the United States abstained from direct interventions in the region. Most clearly, it supported the democratic state of Israel against the helpless Palestinians and the varied authoritarian regimes of Egypt, Jordan and Syria. But it also tried to benefit from the latter's rivalries, facilitating, for instance, a peace agreement between Israel and the military regime in Egypt at the same time that they permitted Syria to invade Lebanon, destroying its democratic regime. The USA supported, on one hand, a despotic monarchy in Saudi Arabia and, on the other hand, the Baath dictatorship in Iraq, an enemy of Saudi Arabia, but one that could act against the Islamic fundamentalists in Iran. However, the USA also helped the Islamic fundamentalists in Afghanistan, friends of those in Iran, facing a Soviet invasion, and so on.

The basic criterion for this labyrinth was to support the foe's rival in order to neutralize it, and then the rival's rival in order to contain it, etc., in order to prevent any one state in the region from becoming sufficiently powerful that it might prevail over the others. The actual outcome of this policy was that the Arab and Muslim world, from Mauritania to Pakistan, was the only region in the world where no democratizing wave ever arrived. Dictatorships of varied inclinations endured and all kinds of conflicts and violence developed. These included long-lasting slaughters between Israelis and Palestinians, several wars of external aggression, like those between Iran and Iraq and the invasion of Kuwait by Iraq, as well as the diffusion, since the 1970s, of transnational terrorism, which eventually led to the attacks in the United States in 2001.

President Bill Clinton had already stated in 1994 that "Ultimately, the best strategy to ensure our security and to build a durable peace is to support the advance of democracy elsewhere. Democracies don't attack each other." After the terrorist attacks in New York and Washington on September 11, 2001, American foreign policy moved first to fighting transnational terrorism and, more ambitiously, to the overarching goal of suppressing all dictatorships in the world. This might indeed be a program for a couple of generations (comparable to the Cold War's length). With this shift, the US government established a strong link between freedom and security in America and freedom in other countries, which implied a break with the tradition of so-called political "realism." As summarized by Secretary of State Condoleezza Rice in 2005: "For 60 years, my country, the United States, pursued stability at the expense of democracy in this region here in the Middle East, and we achieved neither. Now we are taking a different course. We are supporting the democratic aspirations of all people."

The "democratic peace" American foreign affairs doctrine postulates, in essence, that if a ruler is a son of a bitch, he is not ours. Promotion of the American ideals of freedom and democracy is based on the observation that it is the dictatorships that tend to undertake conquest and looting wars, producing mass slaughter and destruction, including so-called "democides" (slaughter with more than one million people dead), both within and outside the dictators' countries. In contrast, democratic regimes rarely start a war of aggression, virtually never fight each other and, in general, minimize political violence. It has been demonstrated that the more democratic a political regime, the lower the probability that it will exert violence whether inside or outside the country. By one account, the interstate wars (again defined as those producing at least one thousand deaths in battle per year and excluding civil wars) from 1816 to 1991 were 198 between dictatorships, 155 between democracies and dictatorships, and zero between democracies (strictly defined).

The most parsimonious explanation of the associations of dictatorship to war and democracy to peace can be based on rulers' self-interest. Typically, democratic governments find relatively great difficulty in obtaining a social consensus to go to war; they face a high probability that the suffering inflicted by war on their citizens will lead to their peaceful, electoral overthrow. Dictatorial governments, in contrast, can usually coerce their subjects into participating in a war and can also expect to obtain direct benefits from the subsequent military gains. In other words: a democratic government will think twice (or more) before participating in an international war, even when it can only be in the interest of political survival. An implication of this is that those wars in which a democratic government participates, usually against a dictatorial government, will likely be won by the former, since if victory were not a reasonable expectation the democratic government would try to avoid the war by all means. After all, this is what dictators and tyrants of all persuasions have repeated again and again: that democracies are too cowardly to venture into certain feats of aggression.

Military relations in the current world are, therefore, dominated by a doctrine that can be labeled, somewhat paradoxically, "idealistic realism." In contrast to the classical "realists," the new vision of US foreign affairs does not see the world as a no man's land open to conquest, nor does it consider that all states are motivated by the same kind of power-seeking ambition that would make them potential rivals and foes. On the contrary, American leaders have distinguished between "good" and "rogue" states, the latter usually put together in some "axis of evil." Instead of aiming at building a "balance of power" among hostile, sovereign states which neutralize each other, it is expected that a country's liberalization and openness will reduce its external aggressiveness. Rather than seeking a peace that is only an absence of world conflict, as in the Cold War times, democratic rulers may pretend to make the great powers' interests coincide with the diffusion of the values of freedom and democracy across the world.

On the other hand, this American foreign policy doctrine does not share the main implication of the so-called "liberal" idealistic tradition, which expected world peace to be a consequence of the prevalence of international law and the central position held by intergovernmental organizations such as the United Nations. Relying upon its extraordinary military strength, the United States may expect to play a universal role of supervision and watch. In this, it openly differs from governments in the European Union, which demand a more active role from international organizations in which they may have greater decision-making power than the proportion of their military contribution would allow.

A crucial point is that the United States' goal to support or establish democratic regimes in the Arab world and the Middle East has been based on the assumption that democracy requires nation–state building. This, however, is not correct, since democratic forms of government have existed and do exist in many small cities, nations and republics not invested with the attribute of sovereignty – as has been noted above and will be further discussed in another chapter. To strengthen states in the Arab region may be a very hard endeavor – especially in the most ethnically heterogeneous countries, Afghanistan, Iraq and Lebanon, which would fit federal-type structures rather well. If sovereign units were strengthened in isolation from each other, a higher degree of "stateness" could, paradoxically, jeopardize the chances of freedom and democracy, since it might revive or foster new inter-state rivalries and mutually hostile relations.

After some initial vacillation, European rulers and NATO members explicitly adopted the American doctrine seeking domestic democracy as the best way to international peace. This decision ultimately derived from the link between domestic democracy and international peace already established in Europe after the Second World War. The main lesson learned from many decades of continuous warfare, especially around the rivalry between France and Germany, was that, in order to prevent new intra-European wars, democratization was a fundamental condition. This has indeed been the permanent message and requirement presented by the European Union to the successive and numerous candidates to join the "club." But democratization and peacemaking in Europe has been successful also thanks to the building of an "imperial" sized Union able to save most states from the task of building their own centralized bureaucracies, armies and borders controls.

Democratization and peacemaking in the Arab world and the Middle East would, therefore, probably be more successful if it ran in parallel to the establishment of large areas of free trade and military and security cooperation. A union of Arab democracies, in several cases organized as federations of smaller units, could be a more effective model than the attempt to build sovereign national states according to the obsolete European model. The Arab League, which was created in the mid 1950s but has never achieved the status of a regular international organization, could perhaps be the embryo of such a network.

Anyway, even if the present democratizing endeavor in the Middle East were to fail, it seems improbable that a new colonialism could develop because the United States at present is a kind of empire without imperialists. American soldiers and chiefs, rather than intending to establish permanent conquests and occupations in order to rule foreign territories directly once they have finished a job – say, for instance, expelling an invading army or overthrowing a dictator – always appear willing to go back home as soon as possible. In contrast to the past empires of Spain, Portugal, Holland, or Britain, which were built on the basis of colonists' emigration from the metropolis, the first military empire in the current world has never been an emigration country, but rather a massive immigration land – actually the main candidate as the adopted homeland of the world's discontents.

6   Market agreements

There is no such thing as "globalization." Almost no market or public good is really "global," in the sense of covering the full area of the earth's "globe." Not even the Gregorian calendar is universally shared; it was enacted by the Pope in the late sixteenth century, but was only much later accepted in most parts of the world, and still now the Moslem and the Persian calendars are regularly used in certain areas. Also weights and measures are still diverse; the USA, for instance, officially adopted the decimal metric system in 1971, but Americans do not care very much. Perhaps the only really worldwide public goods are the world map and the World Wide Web – which are both provided independent of empires, states or nations.

Common standards greatly help human exchanges. The early large area states introduced new common weights, measures and currencies to be used within their borders, which favored the stabilization of large markets. In the current world regular human exchanges develop far beyond the limits of states. But the world is not global (yet?); rather it moves within the areas of several market "empires."

Transnational, not world trade

The transnational circulation of persons, goods, services and capital has increased substantially since the mid-twentieth century. But the relative levels of transnational exchanges at the beginning of the twenty-first century are not very different from those of one hundred years ago. More than worldwide commerce, there is commerce within large economic areas of imperial size, usually called "world regions" by geographers and economists.

Migrations and trade at long distances began to develop on a new larger scale during the nineteenth century with the invention of railways and improvements in navigation, which reduced transport costs to one-fourth of their previous levels within a period of one hundred years. Transnational capital investments, especially from the metropolis to the colonies, were also pushed up by the reduction of communication costs; by the end of the nineteenth century, the entire world was cabled for telegraphy. Thanks to these technical advances, about 60 million people migrated, mostly from Europe to the Americas, between 1850 and the First World War, which amounted to a shift of 3.3 percent of total world population by the end of the period in 1913. The reduction of state-imposed tariffs against private imports of agricultural and industrial products was led by Britain, which was a pioneer in freeing its wheat imports. Most states in continental Europe eventually adopted similar policies and signed treaties favoring commerce. Interest rates in different countries also tended to converge, thus favoring the movement of capitals.

In general, the larger states, which were able to protect internal trade, continued to be relatively more closed externally. The unification of the German territories in the process of creating the modern German state, for instance, involved both the creation of an internal customs union zone (the so-called "Zollverein") and the establishment of a protective common external tariff. The large states or empires of Austria–Hungary, France, Russia, and Spain were externally protectionist. In contrast, in the smaller countries, Belgium, Denmark, the Netherlands, Norway, Sweden and Switzerland, the move towards economic liberalism was more pronounced.

All this progress took place without effective intergovernmental organizations or formal rules, but rather under the protection of the "Pax Britannica," that is, the control of routes by the first imperial power of the time. But the European larger states were colonial rivals and unilaterally sought the conquest of large protected markets not only in the continent of Europe, but also in the rest of the world. At the highest level of economic internationalization, in 1913, the sum of imports and exports accounted for about 30 percent of the world's GDP. But with the turmoil of the First World War and the subsequent outburst of state nationalism, economic protectionism gained adherents. Some large states reintroduced high commercial tariffs and restrictions on immigration and the others retaliated in kind. By the end of the 1920s, the world entered into deep economic depression.

During the period between the First and Second World Wars transnational trade fell by half. It has steadily recovered during the second half of the twentieth century, this time in a more institutionalized setting favoring stability, which includes the International Monetary Fund, the General Agreement on Tariffs and Trade and latterly the World Trade Organization. New reductions in the costs of transport, now especially by air, and of communications, especially by telephone and the internet, have greatly favored these new developments. Trade has increased mainly in industry and services among firms in wealthier nations, rather than in agricultural products from poor countries.

There is a school of thought that persistently labels all this as "unprecedented globalization." This cliché is particularly popular in the United States, probably because the American empire – thanks to its large size – had been relatively protectionist in previous times. But comparisons should be made using the same yardstick. By 2004 the sum of imports and exports was around 35 percent of the world's GDP, that is, only slightly higher, in proportion, than before the First World War. About 104 million people migrated between 1960 and 2000 (of which 35 million went to the United States). This amounts to 1.7 percent of total world population by 2000, that is, still only half the proportion of migrants during the few decades immediately before the First World War.

There is even some accounting illusion in these calculations. When a country splits into two, the former domestic trade is now counted as international trade, and vice versa. This way, "international" trade between, for instance Bavaria and Saxony by the mid-nineteenth century became "domestic" trade a few years later with the creation of a large German state. Analogously, "domestic" trade between, say the regions of Bohemia and Slovakia within the state of Czechoslovakia in 1990, became "international" trade between the Czech Republic and Slovakia a couple of years later. By the same token, domestic companies may suddenly become foreign investors. Similarly, people living in a newly independent state, but born in another state that was previously within the same borders, (say, for instance, Russians in Ukraine) become international migrants at the time of independence without having migrated again.

Since the number of states has tripled since the Second World War, this effect may be significant. There were about 2,500 pairs of states in 1943, but about 20,000 today. If we assume that trade and migration are more likely between neighbors, we could then take into account that there were not many more than 100 bordering neighbors in 1943 and about 400 today. As a consequence of the multiplication of borders, stable amounts of exchanges over time might be counted as an increase in "international" trade.

As mentioned above, large territorial units tend to develop less foreign trade relative to their domestic product than small units. This way, the present economies of the United States or China, for instance, are much less dependent on foreign trade than, say, those of Andorra or Singapore. But this is only another way of saying that within a large state or empire there is extensive "domestic" trade among people and firms located in its different internal "regions," whereas people and firms located in a small independent state can develop similar amounts of trade with traders located at similar distances, but across borders, which counts as "international."

From the point of view of contributing to general welfare, there are no economically meaningful differences between the trade between companies located, for instance, in Illinois and Wisconsin (two "regional" states within the USA), the trade between companies located in Catalonia and Roussillon (two "regions" within different member states of the EU), or the trade between companies located in southern Malaysia and the Riau islands in Indonesia (two parts of two states included in an international trade agreement called the Association of South East Asian Nations, ASEAN). This is so because the tariffs on imports of industrial and manufactured goods within the EU and within the ASEAN are either nil or almost as low as those imposed on domestic commerce within the USA.

It is the borders between nation and nation that make commerce international. The politically interesting implication of this is that a small territorial unit seceding from a large empire or state can be economically viable if, once separated, its companies and individuals can maintain the same amount of trade with traders in its former regional counterparts, whether the latter still belong to the large empire or state or also become independent.

Driven by sectorial specialization and product differentiation, a number of small economic regions emerge within large trade and economic areas. In the USA, there has been a succession of "most prosperous" regions resulting in part from successive new technologies in which they specialize, including New York and the Boston–Washington DC corridor in the northeast; Chicago and Detroit in the midwest with manufacturing and heavy industry; Texas in the south with the oil industry; Los Angeles, San Diego-Tijuana and the San Francisco Bay area on the west coast; and the Pacific Northwest transfrontier Cascadia region, including Seattle and Portland in the US states of Washington and Oregon respectively, and Vancouver in the Canadian province of British Columbia.

In Europe it was traditionally observed that the most prosperous regions were, in addition to those organized around the officially protected large state capitals, those relatively closer within each state to the industrial area around the Rhine and Ruhr rivers in Germany. Nowadays a number of them are experiencing cross-border fertilization, as in Alsace–Lorraine, Northern Italy, Rhône–Alpes, Catalonia and Languedoc–Roussillon.

In China, "special economic zones" have been created from the 1980s on, especially in the provinces of Guandong (including Shenzhen, Zhuhai and Shantou), Fujian (including Xiamen) and Hainan, as well as the Pudong zone in Shangai and other cities in the Yangtze River valley; they expand in parallel to the enclave of Hong Kong. In Japan, emerging economic regions include the cities of Fukuoka and Kitakyushu in the north of the Kyushu Island, Osaka and the Kansai region. Other specialized and growing Asian areas can be identified in Pusan in Southern Korea, as well as in the "growth triangle" formed by Singapore, the southern Malaysian state of Johor and the Riau islands in Indonesia.

The larger the states or the empires, the more regionalized the economic activity tends to be. In general, economic differences across a territory increase with internal integration. For example, the degree of territorial diversification of the economic activity in the United States, due to its long period of internal integration, is much more notable than that within the European Union, where large states still contain some specialized regions that are replicated within other states. But with increasing integration, Europe-wide regional specialization is also increasing. The economic maps of large territories have been compared to an archipelago – the illustration on the cover of this book shows a photograph of the earth capturing those regions with nighttime human activity.

Since the end of the Second World War, although the total amount of transnational trade is increasing, each "imperial" area captures a rather stable share of total world trade. The only economies whose shares of world trade have clearly increased at higher rates than their shares of world production are those of the EU (up to generating more than 40 percent of world trade). But rather than a significant expansion of worldwide commerce, this reflects, of course, the process of integration of the European states and their regions within the continent.

Currencies and agreements

A common market can be identified by the existence of a common price for each commodity or good. Common prices must be based on a common standard, which may be either a common currency or fixed exchange rates among different currencies. Along with the rise of modern states came the establishment of statewide official currencies with the aim of protecting the corresponding markets and increasing trade within state territories. But the unifying force of these decisions has probably been exaggerated since widespread and mutually related regional currencies existed before.

Specifically, in England the "pound sterling," which became the official currency as of 1708, had actually been introduced by the Normans in the eleventh century; in France the *livre tournois* had been used as the kingdom's currency since the thirteenth century, long before the *franc* was established by the revolutionary government in 1795; in Italy, the *lira* had been the basis for the monetary system of numerous cities and principalities on the peninsula since the ninth century, more than one thousand years before the creation of the Italian state; in Spain the different old kingdoms of Aragon, Castile and Navarre maintained their own monetary systems until the nineteenth century, but the *escudo* and the *peso*, or their multiples, were successively used as trade coins several centuries before the creation in 1869 of the *peseta* (a name probably derived from the previous common currency "*peso*"); in Germany the *mark* became the single currency only after unification in 1873, but there were only two basic monetary systems during the previous imperial period, respectively based on the *thaler* (which had also been the currency of the Holy Roman Empire in the north), and the *gulden* in the south. Perhaps it was in the new empire of the USA where independence made a bigger difference in this respect with the creation of the US dollar in 1792, since several foreign coins had been used before.

In medieval and old imperial times the existence of different currencies did not create insurmountable barriers to trade because they referred to common standards. For many centuries, coins were made of gold or silver (or other metals) whose value was determined by the weight of the metal in each coin. Thus, the different small kingdoms, principalities or cities issued coins designed to be used anywhere for their metallic value. In the nineteenth century, both governments and private banks began to issue paper money, but it also had to be backed by gold or silver.

Monetary exchanges existed, therefore, across large territories prior to the establishment of large sovereign states and their official currencies. Also, immediately after the establishment of state official currencies, large international monetary unions were reshaped. They included not only the use of metropolises' currencies in the colonies, but also international agreements like the Latin Monetary Union (gradually including France, Belgium, Greece, Italy, Luxembourg, Spain and Switzerland since 1865) or the Scandinavian Monetary Union (including Denmark, Norway and Sweden from 1875 onward), where the coins of all member countries circulated as legal tender within other member countries.

The expansion of transnational trade during the second half of the nineteenth century examined above was based on respect for the gold standard and the maintenance of fixed exchange rates among all major currencies. This system came to an end during the First World War, when states began to print money without metallic support to finance their massive military expenditures. In the following years, inflation skyrocketed (to the point of multiplying prices by 481 billion times in Germany within a span of five years). For more than thirty years, commerce was replaced by war as the dominant form of interstate exchange.

The gold standard and fixed monetary rates were reestablished at the end of the Second World War, although all currencies were eventually registered in terms of their value relative to the US dollar. But once again, during the 1960s, massive military expenditure, now by the United States for the war in Vietnam, led to printing money, the abandonment in 1973 of the dollar's link to gold (and thus of fixed exchange rates between other currencies), and widespread inflation in the following years.

The diffusion of flexible exchange rates between the different currencies implied that the world economy had ceased to act as a global monetary unit. Logically, it led to the formation of a number of separate currency areas. Previously, the number of currencies in the world had increased together with the number of independent states, from 65 currencies in circulation in 1947 to 169 in 2001 (before the euro was activated). But the number of real monetary systems is nowadays much reduced.

First, the American dollar area includes not only the USA, but also the countries in the so-called Eastern Caribbean area, plus El Salvador and Ecuador, while it is informally but widely used in Mexico and other countries in Central America for high wages, investments and other transactions. Argentina also attached its currency to the US dollar, but in this case the operation failed because the country was at the same time integrated into a customs union (Mercosur) whose partners (mainly Brazil) retained the option to devalue their currencies against Argentine exports. In Asia, the Chinese *yuan renmimbi* was formally pegged to the US dollar until 2005, while other governments, including those of India, Indonesia, S. Korea, Taiwan, Thailand, and even Japan, intervened to peg their currencies to the Chinese or the US currencies in order to prevent excessive fluctuations. Through these unilateral decisions, these governments were supporting relatively cheap Asian exports to the United States.

Second, the European Monetary Union, organized in 1979, led to the creation in 2002 of the euro, which became the official currency of 13 member states of the EU. Another five member states and four candidates to membership maintain either euro-based currency boards or limited flexibility in their currencies with the euro as a reference. Six micro-states have also officially or de facto adopted the euro. Russia and seven other states in Africa and the Middle East hold peg arrangements on currency baskets involving the euro. In West and Central Africa, 14 countries previously enjoying currency agreements with the French *franc* became linked to the euro.

The current world monetary system is, therefore, neither global nor based on fixed rates. Within certain large areas, it allows limited flexibility of exchange rates between currencies. Between areas, the dollar and the euro float freely, which fosters mutual pressures from the governments of the United States, the European Union, China and Japan to make each other appreciate their currencies.

Parallel to the formation of several currency areas, international trade agreements proliferate. It has been observed that, after a few countries establish a customs union or arrive at a preferential or free trade agreement, the countries that remain excluded can benefit more from forming a new, separate trade agreement than from joining the existing one. This produces a proliferation of trade blocs, while the membership size of existing treaties tends to stall.

There were 124 international trade agreements made during the forty-five year period from 1948 to 1994; recently, the process has accelerated: over 130 additional arrangements covering trade in goods and services have been formalized during only the first seven years since the creation of the World Trade Organization in 1995. Some of these agreements are: the European Economic Community in 1957 and the European Free Trade Association in 1960, which merged into the Single-Market Act in 1992 and then the European Union; the Southern Common Market (Mercosur) in the southern cone of the Americas in 1991 and the North American Free Trade Agreement in 1994, both candidates to integrate into the Free Trade Area of the Americas proposed in 1994; the Association of South East Asian Nations, which formed a free trade area in 1992; and the Southern African Development Community and the West African Economic and Monetary Union in 2000.

Virtually no country in the world remains outside some formal international trade agreement, but there is a clear trend toward "imperial"-sized blocs – especially North America, Europe and East Asia. An agreement at the level of an imperial bloc favors intra-bloc trade, especially among a number of specialized small regions. Trade is indeed becoming more concentrated over time within a few large empires of the world. It is not likely that they will completely merge and lead the world economy to global free trade anytime soon.

7   Linguas francas

A language defines a communication area. Most ordinary people live inserted into several communication networks of different widths, which can be organized through different languages. We can speak of "large" and "small" languages depending on the number of people involved. In current times, many individuals share a dual language system formed by some small local language and one or more large "linguas francas." Only a minority of the current world's inhabitants can make it by being monolingual.

The usual encyclopedia information refers to huge numbers of languages and warns of their steadily decreasing numbers (or "language deaths"). Specifically, most reference books give a figure of 4,000 to 5,000 languages in the current world; the latest edition of *Ethnologue* lists and describes 6,912 languages; and almost 40,000 names of languages and dialects have been collected. But this panorama is misleading. It is much more relevant to know that "only" 2,261 languages have writing systems, while the others are only spoken tongues. Only about 300 languages, in fact, have standardized vocabularies and spelling and grammar rules sufficient to produce on-line dictionaries. Just to mention one more criterion of relevance, the United States Department of Education lists 169 languages that are considered worth learning in order to promote research, security or economic exchanges with their speakers (although this has not moved many Americans to become polyglots just yet).

The decrease of the number of languages in the world is, indeed, due to the disappearance of very small non-written languages, including oral tongues spoken by only isolated indigenous communities, as well as several creoles and pidgins. It has been predicted that, out of the several thousand languages registered in the above mentioned lists, about 1,000 or more may likely disappear in a couple of generations and 3,000 or so more are endangered. These numbers closely correspond to those of non-written languages.

Among the written languages, a few very large ones have indeed developed into "linguas francas" of "imperial" extent. Specifically, more than half of the world's population primarily speaks one of 11 large languages: Chinese,

English, Spanish, Hindi, Arabic, Bengali, Russian, Portuguese, Japanese, German and French. As can be seen, these languages closely match the imperial areas identified at the beginning of this book. If we add up all the populations of the countries that have one of these 11 languages as their "official" language, about three-fourths of the world population is included. But at the same time, and as a consequence of broader transnational communications and the new vigor and literacy of a number of local languages, increasing numbers of people have become multilingual.

Creating and abandoning languages

Very many "small" and "large" languages have been created and have disappeared in the history of humankind as a consequence of human migrations and settlements. Humans have alternatively stabilized many local settlements, which produce local tongues, and have launched new waves of dispersion over large territories creating the corresponding common speech.

About ten thousand years ago, most people on earth lived in isolated groups of sedentary gatherers and hunters speaking very small local languages that could be understood by only a few thousand people. Several remnants of that period have been found in modern times. The Aborigines of Australia, for instance, spoke about 270 languages when the Europeans arrived; even today the five million people living on the island of New Guinea speak more than 1,000 languages; there were about 300 American Indian languages in North America, while recent discoveries have identified thousands of languages in the Amazon basin, etc.

But through the expansion of agriculture and territorial conquests, some broad common tongues formed. Farmers took possession of uncultivated land close to that of their forebears and thereby gradually pushed the frontiers of agriculture farther out. This created very large areas of communication in which people spoke in ways that were intelligible to one another. Nevertheless, new local settlements of isolated sedentary farmers and livestock keepers eventually formed. At this new stage, groups of people who spoke nearly the same language again became isolated from each other and after some time they ended up speaking quite differently.

Over time, the spread of successive waves of migration and the expansion of the corresponding common languages has diminished, perhaps counter-intuitively. One reason for this is that when there were very few inhabitants on earth, those who moved about tended to travel across extended territories in search of new resources, while as the number of people on the earth grew, the general tendency was to concentrate in increasingly dense, smaller areas. Thus, a few very large languages spoken by nomadic people became divided into many smaller languages and dialects, which explains the similarities that can be observed between many current languages that are classified within larger linguistic groups. This dispersion of a few large languages into multiple small languages was probably the basis for the biblical myth of Babel: at first, everybody could understand each other, but after a while, like a curse, all began to speak differently.

A few thousands years ago, for instance, those people who are today referred to as "Indo-Europeans" expanded their dominion and influence from a small area somewhere north of the Black Sea to all of Europe and half of Asia. From the so-called Indo-European way of speaking, which was widespread, relatively more isolated but still large Germanic, Slavic, Latin, Greek, Celtic, Persian, Sanskrit and Hindi languages, among others, eventually derived. This means, for instance, that a few centuries before our era, people from England and people from Scandinavia might still to some extent have been able to understand one another's speech. Similarly, the so-called "Sino-Tibetan" language eventually gave way to many Chinese dialects, as well as to the Burmese and the Tibetan languages. Linguists generally recognize about 20 language groups that spread over vast areas and formed separate branches from which most current languages eventually derived. All in all, very many tongues formed and disappeared through successive waves of human migration and settlement across different regions of the world.

The invention of writing changed this path. From that moment on, local languages that were temporarily superseded by an expanding large common language did not inevitably disappear because they could now be empowered by written texts, dictionaries and grammars. A new dual model developed: many people used both a local language that could now survive for a long period if written, and a large lingua franca to communicate within several overlapping areas of different size.

This way, in the Hellenic world, for instance, Greek was the lingua franca for Greeks, Egyptians, Syrians, Phoenicians, Persians and other peoples speaking different languages. Jesus of Nazareth, for example, spoke mostly in Aramaic, the old common language of the Middle East (which is still understood nowadays by people in Iraq, Lebanon, Syria and Turkey), but he probably spoke also in Hebrew with the rabbis in synagogues, as well as in Greek with Pontius Pilate and the other Roman officials, who also spoke Latin.

In the Roman Empire, Latin spread over an area in which possibly more than 100 local languages were spoken. While a few old written languages survived, after AD500 the various forms of spoken Latin in different parts of the old empire also became more and more different. A multitude of local dialects eventually became written languages, including the Castilian, Catalan, Corsican, French, Moldovan, Occitan, Piedmontese, Portuguese, Provencal, Rhaeto-Romance, Romaine, Sardinian and Tuscan languages. For several centuries, a dual language system remained stable: Latin was the lingua franca for international contact and higher education, while a number of old pre-Latin and new Latin-derived local languages prevailed in daily life and small-area communications and exchanges.

Similarly, the Germanic language eventually gave way to, among others, the relatively close Afrikaans, Alemannic-Swabian, Austro-Bavarian, Bokmål (Dano-Norwegian), Danish, Dutch, English, Flemish, Frisian, Middle German, Icelandic, Luxembourgian, Nynorsk (New Norwegian), Saxon, Swedish, and Yiddish, just to name a few of the written languages. Analogously, from Slavic, differently spoken languages were codified as Belarusian, Bulgarian, Croatian, Czech, Macedonian, Polish, Russian, Serbian, Slovak, Slovenian, Ukrainian and others. While a few of these languages tended to become languages for large-scale communication, writing allowed the other languages to also survive at local level.

State monolingualism

The hitherto unknown ambition to make everybody within a large territory monolingual was typical of the monopolistic projects of a number of modern European states. To achieve this, each state had to choose one single language, usually the variety used in the state capital, and make it compete with both the several local languages spoken within the state territory and with Latin – the extant lingua franca which continued to be used for centuries by the Catholic church in worship and education.

New standard grammars and rules were defined from the sixteenth century onward for each sovereign-state language to make it sharply differentiated from neighboring state languages with the same origin. Neighboring peoples living on either side of state borders became increasingly unable to understand each other. Each of the new large states diffused the norms of one single language by using the state administration, the new invention of printing, the expansion of schooling as well as instruction during military service, the admission of only one language in correspondence and telephony, and through several forms of persecution and repression of other languages.

Specifically, at the time of the French revolution in the late eighteenth century hardly half of the citizens of France spoke standard French, but the generalization of the single official language was achieved by the end of the nineteenth century. Less than three percent of Italian citizens could speak standard Italian at the moment of the creation of the Italian state in the late nineteenth century. And not so long ago, pupils of France, Spain and Sweden, for instance, could be severely punished if they spoke their parents' language rather than the official state language during breaks in school.

The fulfillment of this ambition was, however, not always complete. Actually, many people who, as a consequence of the state's norms and indoctrination, think they are speaking different languages can still understand one another to a significant extent. In many cases, the difference between a dialect and a language is a question of official criteria rather than of linguistic distance. Portuguese people, for instance, understand Spaniards pretty well, as Brazilians can understand Argentines (although not so much the other way around), but they certainly think they are speaking a different language, mainly because they belong to different states. Even Galician, a very close variant of Portuguese but spoken outside the state borders of Portugal, was formalized as a different language by newly emerging Galician nationalist movements during the second half of the twentieth century. Similarly, Swedes and Norwegians understand each other well and usually maintain bilingual conversations, but they also established their ways of speaking as different languages when they formed separate states. The same has happened, for instance, between Czechs and Slovaks. Serbs and Croats believed they spoke different, the same, and again different languages at different moments during the twentieth century, respectively before, during and after the existence of multinational Yugoslavia. In general, state borders, distance, and isolation, together with the ambition of holding mutually exclusive state sovereignties, increase the differences between languages which have the same origin. Nowadays, even a typical East Londoner can hardly understand a fellow from Texas; as George Bernard Shaw put it, "England and America are two countries separated by the same language."

Conquests and voyages over the seas did indeed impose English and other European languages on America and Australia. But in other parts of the world the failure of the state project has also implied a failure in imposing one single language. Most people in Southern Asia, Africa, Central America and the Andean region still speak any one of the many languages that existed before the arrival of Europeans. The official state languages, which were imposed by the colonial metropolis, are regularly spoken in private conversations by only parts of the populations.

A multilingual world

Most people of the world are bilingual or multilingual. Some of the larger empires and federal states, including, for instance, the United States and Germany, do not have official languages. About 30 percent of states give official recognition to more than one language, while sizeable small groups also speak non-official languages in officially monolingual countries. The persistence of small languages for daily life and small-area communication, together with the insufficient communication capability provided by each official state language, has given way to the diffusion of new linguas francas and the search for a world language.

English is certainly the most successful transnational language in the current world. Although the success of the English language largely derives from the political and military success of two successive English-speaking empires, Britain and America, its wide reach has made English a de-ethnicized and culture-unbounded language allowing many of its speakers to use it freely without identifying with one particular country. In America, and in contrast to state languages in Europe, English never achieved the mythic category of the "official" or "national" language. For those speaking English as a foreign language, it works in a similar way to how Latin worked as the lingua franca for the learned community for many centuries. English has become the worldwide lingua franca not only in higher education and academic publications and conferences, it is dominant in science, technology and medicine, in international business, finance and commerce, and in diplomacy. It's also the language of airports, sports, pop music and advertising.

Beyond being the mother tongue of more than 400 million people, English is official or semi-official in over sixty countries and has a prominent place in another twenty. In Europe, English may appear to many as a more "neutral" language than, say, French or German and is indeed very popular as a foreign language. In particular, English is regularly spoken by most of the adult population in the Scandinavian countries and the Netherlands – although certainly not at the expense of Swedish, Norwegian, Danish, Finnish or Dutch. English may develop a similar attraction in other parts of the world. In Latin America, it has no rival for learned individuals. In total, people able to speak English as either a first or foreign language might amount up to one-fourth of the world's population.

However, English is not the only large-area lingua franca in the large empires of the present world. In China, the common written language acts as the standard over a continuum of Chinese dialects that includes the majority Mandarin together with Wu, Cantonese, Min, Hsiang and Hakka (with differences as notable as those between, say, different Latin-derived languages in Europe), as well as many others derived from the Tai, Turkic, Tibeto-Burman and other language groups. In India, both Hindi and English work as linguas francas for a population speaking more than a dozen officially recognized languages and more than 30 additional languages which each have more than one million speakers, languages derived from Sanskrit, Dravidian, Munda, Tibeto-Burman and other language groups. In Pakistan, Urdu is the semi-official, although minority language for people speaking Punjabi, Sindhi, Pashto and other languages. In Indonesia, the former colonial language, Dutch, was replaced not with one of the widely spoken languages, like Javanese or Sudanese, but with the Bahasa-Indonesian adapted from Malayan, which was a more neutral choice because it was the first language of only a small minority; education is bilingual, taking place in both the new lingua franca and one of more than twenty local languages with a broad following.

In North Africa and the Middle East, Arabic is the lingua franca for education, administration and the media, while spoken dialects are quite varied, including Algerian, Egyptian, Iraqi, Lebanese, Moroccan, Palestinian, Saudi, Sudanese and Syrian; other local languages are also increasingly used, like Berber and Kurd. In Africa, the neutral languages of the former colonialists, especially English and French, are official in many countries and widely used, while Swahili is also widespread in West and Central Africa as the lingua franca for speakers of hundreds of small local languages.

International and large-scale communication can be achieved by either concentrating on a single lingua franca, like English, or by individual multilingualism. It has been calculated that two persons with different first languages but who are bilingual will in at least half the cases share a common language chosen at random among a set of six languages. For trilingual individuals the probability of a common language rises to around 90 percent in a context of ten or more languages. This means that if every individual, in addition to speaking his own local language, learned two additional languages selected from among a few linguas francas, the possibility of human understanding would be almost guaranteed.

8 Small democracies

Small nations not only have new opportunities to be viable in the current world without the need to belong to large sovereign states. They also are better positioned for improvements in democracy. In order to explain the formation of increasing numbers of small political units, the "opportunity" created by transnational developments such as those reviewed in the previous chapters can be considered a necessary but not a sufficient condition. The development of large military, commercial and cultural empires makes small nations "viable," but does not explain their formation or existence. The decentralization of large states and small nations' independence results more directly from processes driven by political demands and strategies; they are not a mechanical consequence of structural changes.

The basic motivation for those promoting or favoring the organization of small political units is derived from the high costs of aggregating preferences and making collective decisions in large states, costs that are levied on citizens and leaders as political defeats, discrimination or exclusion, with the corresponding protests and demands. A new aspect of the situation is that, in the current world, decentralizing or seceding democratic strategies, which might always have had sound motives for many people living in large states, nowadays involves lower military, economic and communication costs and becomes, thus, more appealing. Small community self-government is today possible without an army, borders or customs.

The advantages of small units for democracy

That a small community is more appropriate than a large and populous territory for a democratic form of self-government is a very old postulate. Already on the basis of the classical experience of Athens, philosopher Aristotle stated that a political community (*polis*) should be sufficiently small so that the citizens could know one another and assemble at one place to hear speakers and participate directly in deliberations on public matters. As recently as the eighteenth century, prominent thinkers like Montesquieu and Rousseau associated democracy only with cities and small countries, contrasting them to the pairing of mixed monarchies and tyrannical empires with large and very large territories respectively. Montesquieu, in particular, identified three basic types of advantages for a small community in terms of good governance, which we will revise in the light of current developments: "In a small democracy," he said, "the public good is more strongly felt, better known, and closer to each citizen." Looking at the question from the other side, this idea suggests that in a large state, people may receive less and more deficient information on the set of policy issues submitted to collective decision-making and feel more distant from government.

The disadvantages large unitary states have in establishing a democracy able to satisfy the preferences of a large majority of its citizens are not difficult to identify. Within a large political unit, different interests, values, and opinions are likely to exist among the citizens. A collective decision made on a set of different policy issues en bloc is likely to produce a high number of losers. In a single election, voters have to choose a single "package" of policies, regarding, for instance, the economy, social issues, schooling, foreign affairs, etc., more or less like consumers who have to choose a single-brand package of products in a supermarket instead of filling their baskets with freely chosen goods. Local majorities may then become state-wide minorities on many issues and see their preferences excluded from binding collective decisions. In contrast, small political units permit different groups of people, each with relatively homogeneous preferences, to make decisions à la carte. The total number of individuals who can see their preferences satisfied by governmental decisions is higher if the population is organized into a set of many small units each making their own decisions than if it does so in a single large unit.

In the extreme, dictatorships will be more likely to emerge and triumph in very large political units (or in highly heterogeneous ones). A dictatorship implies, by definition, that imperative decision making is not based on citizens' preferences, but on the dictator's. Since the costs of aggregating citizens' preferences and making compelling and enforceable collective decisions tend to increase with the size of the political unit and the heterogeneity of the population, effective decision making by dictatorial means finds more acceptance – even if only in a resigned and passive way – in larger communities where attempts to aggregate disparate citizen's preferences by fair procedures is more costly. In other words, if the citizens in a large community have extremely diverse preferences and interests, the difficulty in forming a consistent majority able to make effective decisions may result in collective paralysis and chaos, which may lead some to accept dictatorship as a lesser evil.

A large, heterogeneous society with several lines of conflict and lower internal cohesion may create, thus, more opportunities for a dictator to raise and win than would a small, homogeneous community with dense networks of human relations. Also, for a potential dictator motivated by confiscatory aims, the existence of a very large colonial dominion or a very large territory under a single jurisdiction may be a relatively appealing setting, since he might extract a higher total volume of income from a large population than in a scarcely populated country. However, the larger the country, the more costly the administrative and police apparatus needed to keep the dictator in control, so effective dictatorships should also have a limited size. Actually a single dictator-ruled world empire has never existed nor does one seem likely to arise.

More precisely, the advantages of small communities for democratic government can be found in each of the three stages of the decision process: deliberation, aggregation and enforcement. They include:

- *Deliberation* In a small community, citizens have more opportunities to gain knowledge for collective decision making by direct observation and experience. Thanks to territorial proximity, citizens can also deal more directly with political leaders; the latter can easily gain information about citizens' demands and expectations by direct communication.
- *Aggregation* A small community tends, in general, to be relatively homogeneous in terms of both economic and ethnic variables, so that its citizens have relatively similar occupations, levels of education, income and wealth levels, as well as commonalities in religion, race and language. Citizens may also have relatively harmonious interests, shared values and a common culture – or, in more technical terms, consensual preferences and shared criteria of choice. All this may make it easier for the citizens to identify priority public goods and make collective decisions that are generally acceptable.
- *Enforcement* Small communities are more likely to generate loyalty. People will tend to comply with collective rules and decisions while leaders may be more responsive regarding their own decisions and activities.

On the other hand, small communities may be victims of parochialism and a narrow perspective on possible alternatives to the issues submitted to collective decision. This aspect of localistic narrowness is the one that has usually been stressed in a certain statist tradition. But innovation can develop in a small nation under conditions of openness which naturally derive from its membership of a large area of imperial size.

The old tradition of local self-government

There is a very old tradition of local self-government in many places in Europe and the Americas – and probably in other less publicized parts of the world. In ancient, medieval and early modern times, there was an array of small units where many collective decisions were made by the vote of a broad electorate, including villages, communes, municipalities, republics, provinces, counties, towns, boroughs, colonies, or other communities of small size. The better known cases include the Swiss rural villages and cantons that have existed since the late Middle Ages, as well as a number of medieval Italian communes like Bergamo, Bologna, Florence, Genoa, Lucca, Pavia, Pisa, Siena or Venice. Initially, the medieval commune in Central Europe assumed the administration of justice, military defence, maintenance of the food supply and other basic services. To the extent that the counts and the bishops were unable to perform these tasks effectively, the cantons and communes gradually replaced their authority. Eventually, they ignored the sovereignty of the German emperor or the Roman pope. In the course of this process, the Helvetic Confederation of Switzerland was created and is still a prominent instrument in preserving local popular self-government.

Elsewhere, many self-governing units were absorbed by the new large states. Certain extensive kingdoms temporarily respected towns' and provinces' autonomy and kings summoned assemblies elected in small, local and homogeneous districts. Many French municipalities in the Southern Occitanie, including Montpellier and Nimes, developed genuine forms of self-government. Provincial estates and the Estates-General in pre-revolutionary Bourbon France also used broad suffrage to vote on taxes, loans, and expenses. In Hanoverian England, town meetings and shire courts were called periodically to settle disputes, proceed with judicial matters, and choose tax collectors. Towns and boroughs elected delegates to represent their interests in the county courts. The parliament summoned by the king was also elected in small shires and counties, cities and urban boroughs.

One of the earliest meetings recorded of a representative assembly in Europe was held in Barcelona in the early eleventh century for the approval by consensus and acclamation of public laws later compiled in the celebrated "Customs" of the city. Local government also became the basis for the formation of wider representative parliaments. The Courts of Catalonia and Aragon were summoned by the king to regular assemblies of representatives of the clergy, the nobles, and the knights, as well as the towns, from the mid-twelfth century. The Catalan Courts, in particular, were called regularly "to treat of matters of common utility for the country" and the king committed himself and his descendants to enact any general decision made with the "approval and consent" of the citizens. Eventually these and many other similar experiences were curbed by an increasingly centralized control, which usually also implied the disenfranchisement of certain voting groups or simply the suppression of all types of elections.

One institutional invention was crucial in making democracy workable for large populations. When, in the late eighteenth century, 13 small, highly homogeneous communities in North America began to gain independence from the United Kingdom, they invented a federation of small republics, thus making large size and democracy compatible for the first time. In this way, the United States of America was actually created not as a large sovereign state, but as a large federation of small democratic units, or a democratic empire – in the sense defined at the beginning of this book.

Outside the framework of a large federation, small nations in modern history have hardly been self-sufficient, while being highly vulnerable to external attacks or absorption by large states. But in the current world of "imperial" military alliances, large open markets and broad linguas francas, small democracies, even those not attached to a tight federation, have again become viable and, as always, advantageous in comparison to extensive, heterogeneous states.

Small is democratic

The modern spread of democracy in the world has coincided with and has somehow derived from a dramatic increase in the number of independent countries and the corresponding decrease in their size, as well as the concurrent decentralization of large empires and states. With a decrease in the size of the political unit, the likelihood of durable freedom and democracy increases.

In the late nineteenth century, competitive elections to legislative assemblies by universal male (and female in only one case) suffrage were regularly established in only nine of 52 empires and states existing at the time. In other words, about a century ago, electoral democracy existed in only one-sixth of the extant states, an area in which less than ten percent of the total population lived; most humankind lived in authoritarian monarchies or empires or under colonial domination. Specifically, democratic elections with broad suffrage were introduced for the first time with relatively durable results in France in 1871, Switzerland in 1875, the United States in 1879, the United Kingdom in 1886, New Zealand in 1890, Canada in 1891, Spain in 1891, Norway in 1897, and Belgium in 1900.

In contrast, by the early twenty-first century democracy characterized by high levels of civil liberties and competitive elections in which both men and women vote exists (in 2006) in 89 countries, in which 45 percent of the world's population (and 55 percent of all people outside China) lives – almost half of the 198 currently recognized countries. In other words, in little more than a century, from 1900 to 2006, while the number of countries in the world has quadrupled, the number of democracies has increased by a factor of ten. The proportion of countries with democratic regimes has thus increased by a factor of two and a half; the proportion of the world's population living in democracy by a factor of five.

Non-democratic regimes may be distinguished as dictatorial and semi-democratic (the latter holding regular elections for significant offices but with restrictions either on suffrage or the degree of electoral competition). Looking only at strict dictatorships, the proportion of the world's population under this type of regime is currently about one third (mostly concentrated in the Arabic or Muslim countries in North Africa and the Middle East), which is about half the proportion of one hundred years ago.

The waves by which increasing numbers of independent nations were created, as discussed in the first part of this book, developed very closely alongside successive waves of democratization. It is relevant to note that the existence of very large colonial empires was traditionally considered incompatible not only with freedom for the colonized peoples but also with liberalization and democratization of the metropolitan state. Already in the eighteenth century, the liberal Adam Smith dreamed that "Great Britain should voluntarily give up all authority over her colonies, and leave them to elect their own magistrates, to enact their own laws, and to make peace and war as they might think proper," in order to save military expense and develop more advantageous free trade. The radical democrat Jeremy Bentham, who had also favored relinquishing the British colonies in North America, sent a message to the French National Convention proposing "Emancipate your colonies!"; later on, he advised the Spanish liberal constituents to "Rid themselves of Ultramaria," that is, of the Central and South American colonies, in the cause of adopting a more democratic regime in Spain. Even the socialist Karl Marx, although he was more ambiguous regarding the "civilizing" effects of colonialism in Asia, hoped that the "emancipation of the English working class" would be greatly favored by the independence of Ireland from Britain. Indeed, both Great Britain and Spain, although at very different paces, only began to introduce stable universal suffrage and competitive elections by ridding themselves of most of their colonies – therefore reducing their "size" and the heterogeneity of the population under their dominion.

But democratization advanced significantly not only as a consequence of the reduction in size of the larger empires, but as a consequence of the dissolution of some of these empires and the corresponding creation of small independent nations. A number of new democracies were established at the beginning of the twentieth century and in the aftermath of the First World War, when several old European empires fell and a number of new states were created. However, virtually all of these new democratic regimes disappeared as a consequence of communist revolutions and fascist counter-revolutions during the 1920s and 1930s. At the beginning of the Second World War in 1939 the number of democracies was about the same as forty years before. Democratization spread more widely after 1945, first with the liberation of Western Europe, (including France, Germany and Italy), and Japan, and also with the further independence of many colonies and the formation of new countries in Africa and Asia, including the early instances of India and Israel. By the late 1960s, while the number of recognized countries had almost tripled, the number of democracies had multiplied by five. The proportion of countries with democratic regimes had, thus, nearly doubled in less than 30 years.

The so-called third wave of democratization started in Southern Europe in 1974, including Portugal, Greece, and Spain, moved to Latin America, including Argentina, Brazil, and Chile, moved to a few countries in Africa and Asia in the 1980s, and spread more dramatically to Central and Eastern Europe, including Poland, Hungary and a number of new republics, such as the Baltics, in the 1990s. Relatively stable communist dictatorships had been established in 15 countries with almost 40 percent of the total world's population. The disintegration of the Soviet Union, Yugoslavia and Czechoslovakia and the fall of communism in Central Europe transformed nine of those states into 26, of which today more than half are democracies and others are in intermediate, partly free conditions trying to move towards increasing liberalization.

During this period, in which most of the world's current democracies have been established, several "imperial"-sized organizations openly facilitate democratization and the survival of democracy. The NATO, the Organization for Security and Cooperation in Europe, and the European Union, as well as the Organization of American States, the North American Free Trade Agreement and Mercosur, have effectively pressured member states or aspiring candidates to democratize or to redemocratize after reversals to authoritarian rule. It is, thus, a new type of "imperial," non-state network providing collective defense and security, as well as free trade agreements and other large-scale public goods that aid the existence and democratization of small nations, in contrast to the authoritarian uses of traditional colonial domination.

Globally, during the last 30 years, while the number of countries in the world has increased by a half, the number of democracies has more than doubled. The correlation between small size and democracy is, thus, consistent, since the creation of increasingly numerous, smaller countries has accompanied the spread of democratic regimes. Nowadays, there is democracy in almost all recognized micro-countries with less than 300,000 inhabitants, in more than two-thirds of those with less than one million inhabitants (including the former group), and in more than half of all small countries with less than 10 million inhabitants (including the two former groups), while only one third of large countries with more than 10 million inhabitants enjoy democratic regimes (specifically, there is democracy in 59 of the 112 smaller countries, but in only 30 of the 86 larger countries). In other words, the number of small democracies is twice the number of large democracies.

The rates of success in democratization are even higher for small communities within large federalized states or empires. In addition to the early experiences of democratic federalism in the United States and Switzerland already mentioned, other newly independent states with large and disparate territories adopted federal-type structures, including Canada in 1867, Brazil in 1891, Australia in 1901 and India in 1947. Federalism and decentralization has also developed together with democratization or democratic renewal in Germany since 1949, Belgium and Italy since 1970, Spain since 1977 and South Africa in 1994, along with other countries using diverse territorial formulas.

Nowadays, of all the large countries in the world with more than 10 million inhabitants, those with a federal structure are democratic in almost *three-fourths of cases*, while in large centralized and unitary states, democracy only exists in *one-fourth* of cases (specifically, there is democracy in 13 of 18 large federal countries, but in only 17 of 68 large centralized states). Decentralization and federalism, which give small nations and regions means of self-government, consolidate democracy. No backsliding towards authoritarianism has existed in recent times in plural federations which have adopted democratic formulas. When multiple small political units have been established in a large territory, they effectively resist further attempts at centralization and concentration of power. In a few very large dictatorial empires (like China, Russia, or Pakistan), the demands and expectations of decentralization have become synonymous with democratization. While dictatorship affirms itself by means of concentrating power in the center, resistance to authoritarian rule always involves more transparent and accountable local self-government.

Part III

The European empire

One may hear that the institutional formulas of the European Union are "unique," "exceptional" or "unprecedented." This is indeed a frequent assertion in certain journalistic literature and political speech. For a social scientist, however, this only means that we are not using a sufficiently broad analytical concept, capable of including this case among those with common relevant characteristics. The appropriate concept could be that of "empire," as defined at the beginning of this book. The EU is indeed a very large political unit (with the third largest population in the current world), it has expanded continuously outward, it is organized diversely across the territory and has multiple, overlapping institutional levels of governance, as will be analyzed in the following chapter.

As is typical of empires, the EU has no fixed territorial limits. The initial European Community, which had six member states in 1957, has gradually enlarged, up to 27 members in 2007, and there are still more than a dozen potential candidates for membership. The territorial limits for an empire are only those of another empire. In this case a logical limit should be Russia, which has been shrinking since the dissolution of the Soviet empire in 1991. But the EU might stop its fifty-year process of steady expansion short of the limits of that empire, which would produce frustrated expectations and perhaps significant discontent and instability among the excluded.

Other Europe-wide organizations have indeed expanded beyond the present limits of the EU. They include, in particular, two organizations that contributed actively to the democratization of the south and the east of the continent: the Council of Europe, encompassing the "wider Europe" of 46 member states, and the Organization for Security and Cooperation in Europe, with 55 members (including two in North America). For quite different purposes, the Union of European Football Associations (UEFA) assembles participants from 52 countries, while the Eurovision Song Contest has gathered participants from up to 39 countries, most of the additional ones also potential candidates for the EU.

9 Unity in diversity

Among the fundamental elements of the European Union are the three dimensions of imperial and transnational human relations that were revised in the second part of this book: military alliances, trade agreements and linguas francas for communication. Indeed the imperial-sized EU has permitted the parallel development of large markets and regional economic specialization, broad communication and plural cultures, inclusive federal structures and small democratic institutions.

A security alliance

As for most empires, the initial project of what is today the EU involved strong military motivations. Similar to the way the creation of the USA, for example, was conceived by the newly independent small communities in the late eighteenth century, mainly as a mechanism for self-protection from the former colonial power and other foreign threats, so there were, for reasons of security, also strong military reasons for the initial project of building the United States of Europe. The union of Europe was promoted by the mid-twentieth century mainly as a reaction to frequent and highly lethal wars between large states, usually involving France and Germany, as well as domestic civil wars and political instability, culminating in the Second World War. As the most powerful European states lost their colonies overseas, their military and economic union in Europe could also be conceived of as a new kind of common empire. The continuing expansionist policy of the imperial Soviet Union, as demonstrated by the occupation and domination of Central Europe, and most dramatically by the division of Germany, also reinforced the incentives for West European states to create a common defense and security system, in addition to their reliance on the military protection of the United States.

The union of Europe thus began as a military enterprise. After the establishment of the North Atlantic Treaty Organization (NATO), led by the United States, in 1949, a first attempt was made to create a European Defense Community, which failed. A second attempt, more explicitly under NATO's umbrella, was the creation of the Western European Union in 1954.

In parallel, a number of economic agreements among several European states were conceived as a means to reduce competition for strategic resources, such as coal, steel and atomic energy, and in this way to prevent some of the most critical causes of war.

As happened with the six founding members of the European Community in 1957, additional members also had significant reasons, based on previous wars, to apply for membership. Southern European countries sought European membership as a guarantee against the reemergence of past military dictatorships. Other recent new members and possible candidates for European membership have proved to be nonviable states outside a large empire. Most of them were victims of either the German expansion in the early 1940s, or the further Soviet expansion at the end of the Second World War, or both. Certain Eastern European countries have passed almost directly from being members of the Soviet Union to being members of the European Union (like the three Baltic republics); others have historically belonged to a number of successive empires (like Cyprus). When riots and threats of civil war have exploded in bordering states, the EU has promoted their liberalization and democratization (as happened in the Balkans and some former republics of the Soviet Union). Membership to the EU creates economic and political links able to prevent future military conflicts. For almost all countries, membership of the EU is also linked to membership of NATO and other Western military alliances.

Specialized markets

After the initial momentum, further progress towards an "ever closer" union, as mentioned in the founding Treaty of Rome, has been driven by the aim of aggregating resources by trade rather than by direct military initiatives. The economically based union of Europe has been highly successful in diffusing the benefits of free trade, in this way preventing the emergence of motives for new wars between member states of the union, but also promoting significant prosperity and well-being.

With successive enlargements and gradual economic integration of the Union, the degree of economic diversity across the European territories has increased and will likely increase much more in the future. To understand this general economic trend it may be helpful to compare the EU with the USA. Consider, for instance, the case of a relatively recent industry, the automobile industry. In the USA, the automobile developed during the second third of the twentieth century within an already unified large market, with a common currency, free of tariffs and other barriers to trade. This large-area economic integration facilitated the development of a single dominant automobile producing region in southern Michigan (especially in the city of Detroit) and the neighboring states of Indiana and Ohio, which over time took advantage of its early development to increasingly reinforce the territorial concentration of the industry.

In contrast, the development of the automobile industry in Europe at about the same time took place within statewide, protected markets. The result was that Britain, France, Germany, Italy, even Spain all had their own automobile industries. At the beginning of the twenty-first century, the automobile industry is still more evenly spread across the European territory than across the United States. But as international markets become more integrated, as is happening within the EU, each region tends to specialize in a few key activities and to sell to broader markets. Just as it happened in the USA, we should, therefore, expect that there will be in the future Europe not only one or two automobile producing regions, but also one increasingly dominant financial center (probably London, or perhaps also Frankfurt), one center for aircraft manufacturing (growing in Toulouse), a few agricultural regions (particularly in Poland and some highly specialized areas), some preferential areas for tourism (especially the Mediterranean) and so on.

Admittedly, the forces of uneven development may change over time. In particular, falling transportation costs may reduce the incentive for firms to concentrate together and favor, instead, their spreading out in order to improve their access to markets. But within a broad common market with a common currency, regions that have been closely interrelated within a state may not necessarily be each other's main trading partners in the future. With the loss of their sovereignty, the European states have ceased to be cohesive economic units. With open borders, state-peripheralized and bordering regions tend to escape state control.

Increasing regional economic differentiation across Europe may not necessarily produce higher income inequalities if many regions specialize in different advantageous things – regional inequalities are in fact relatively small within the highly integrated and specialized United States. But increasing territorial differentiation is likely to give support to increasingly differentiated sectoral and territorial demands, which should also lead to varied forms of institutional decentralization.

Dual plurilingualism

Europe is a very multilingual empire where an array of local, statewide and transnational languages coexist with a few linguas francas. In the EU with 27 member states there are 40 languages that are spoken by at least 300,000 people (which is the number of people speaking the smallest of the state and EU official languages, Maltese). These languages are: Basque, Breton, Bulgarian, Catalan, Corsican, Croatian, Czech, Danish, Dutch, English, Estonian, Finnish, Flemish, French, Frisian, Friulian, Gaelic, Galician, German, Greek, Hungarian, Italian, Latvian, Lithuanian, Luxembourgish, Maltese, Occitan, Polish, Portuguese, Romanian, Romance, Russian, Sardinian, Serbian, Slovak, Slovenian, Spanish, Swedish, Turkish and Welsh, aside from about one dozen smaller languages.

In 23 of the 27 member states of the EU several languages are spoken. The only states that can be considered virtually monolingual are the Czech Republic, Denmark, Hungary and Portugal. There may be about 30 million people in Europe whose first language is not the first official language of the state.

In search of a common language, most Europeans have skipped the old rivalry between French and German and have favored English as a third, more neutral language. Reticence towards the two former languages was fed by attempts to impose one single dominant language across Europe. As a prelude to further imperialistic attempts, the philosopher Voltaire, for instance, had declared that "the French language is the most general of all languages of Europe, because it is the best suited for conversation." The philosopher Fichte, for his own part, had similarly held that German was the only truly European language because "the others have been sought by strange languages." In contrast to the norm in large states, the name of the state where English is the major language, the United Kingdom of Great Britain, does not correspond to the name of the language.

More than half of Europeans can speak one additional language and more than one-fourth, two additional languages. The number of speakers of English as a first language in Europe is lower than those of French or German and, precisely on this basis, the number of Europeans able to speak English is triple that of native English speakers – a proportion much higher than those for the other two languages mentioned. About half of the total population in Europe can speak English either as a first language or as an additional language, while about one-third can speak German and one-fourth can speak French. In countries such as Denmark, the Netherlands and Sweden, more than 80 percent of the people can speak additional languages, in almost all cases including English. In all European countries, the number of students of English as a foreign language is increasing.

The institutions of the EU recognize 23 languages as official, basically corresponding to the official state languages (although the list does not include Luxembourgish and Gaelic-Irish had been added only by 2007). In the European Parliament and the European Commission, however, English and French act as linguas francas. Communication between EU officers and the media is regularly done in English, French and German, followed only sometimes by Dutch, Italian, Polish and Spanish. Some of the 23 official languages are not even used for publishing official documents or for simultaneous translation (imagine the difficulties in finding professional translators between, say, Estonian and Greek or Maltese and Finnish).

There are other selections of linguas francas at the European level. The TV channel Euronews, for example, broadcasts in seven languages: English, French, German, Italian, Portuguese, Russian and Spanish, which can be selected by just clicking on the remote control. In the popular Eurovision Song Contest, a broad variety of languages has also been used, including not only the states' official languages, but also Breton, Catalan, Corsican,

Romance and several minor languages. But since contestants have been permitted since 1999 to choose what language they will sing in, all seven successive winners have come from non-English speaking countries but have sung in English.

All in all, the EU has become a very good example of the dual linguistic model developed by classical empires. A few large linguas francas supersede but do not eliminate the multiple local languages, which is a far cry from the monopolistic ambition of sovereign states to impose one single language within a given territory.

10 Self-government à la carte

Within the European Union, small political units proliferate and adopt varied institutional formulas. Two thirds of the member states of the Union are small units with less than 10 million inhabitants. At the same time, the five larger states, Germany, France, Britain, Italy and Spain, plus two others of intermediate size, Belgium and Austria, are federal or increasingly decentralized states. In total, more than 70 non-state small political units with legislative assemblies and executive governments exist within the territory of the EU. In other states there are powerful municipal governments and other territorial administrative structures.

The basic institutional formulas are diverse across the territory. Of the 27 member states of the EU, 20 are republics, but seven are monarchies; 22 are parliamentary regimes in which the executive is chosen by the parliament, but in five others the president is directly elected and has significant executive powers; most countries are multiparty and have proportional representation electoral rules, but two still use electoral systems based on the majority principle and two have adopted mixed systems. Among the smaller political units within large states, the diversity of institutional and political formulas is even greater; actually, there is a positive correlation between the degree of local self-government and the local units' capacity to choose institutional formulas different from those used in the state at large. Transnational cooperation develops not only among regions within traditional large states, but also across state borders, leading to the formation of euro-regions and leagues of non-neighboring regions. The large umbrella of the EU creates incentives for peaceful self-government and the cooperation of small political units that had previously been in conflict within the choking limits of sovereign states.

The example of Federal Germany

The Federal Republic of Germany may be the best example of federal relations among a number of small political units within a large state. This is largely due to the fact that federalism was established in Germany with the aim of weakening the German state and favoring territorial governments. At the end of the Second World War, only the occupying Soviets desired a strong, unified government, which they eventually established on their own as a communist dictatorship in the eastern part of the territory. In the rest of the territory, by contrast, priority was given to the creation of new democratic land governments by the occupying powers of America, Britain and France. In the words of the American Secretary of State at the time, a strong state was not desirable because "it could be too readily converted to the domination of a regime similar to the Nazis;" thus, as it was put by the British Foreign minister, "all powers should be vested in the lands except such as are expressly delegated to the central government;" his French colleague went so far as to conceive of the center as a mere "coordination" of lands with the national parliament consisting only of a chamber of lands. No defense powers, in particular, were initially recognized in the new German government.

First, there were elections for 11 land parliaments and governments in the western part of Germany. The lands approved their own constitutions, in some cases officially establishing a "free state." It was the lands who appointed a "parliamentary council" in charge of drafting a democratic constitution to establish a governmental structure of the federal type in 1949. The lands were given exclusive powers over police, local government, education, cultural and religious affairs, and in control of the assessment and collection of all major taxes, as well as concurrent powers in other domains. The lands could modify their borders and, in fact, three of them merged in 1952. Recent institutional reforms tend to allocate more exclusive powers to both the federal government and the land governments, which may foster interterritorial competition but also self-government.

Fifty years later, after the reunification with the eastern part of the country, the number of lands grew to 16, ranging from the free states of Bavaria, Saxony and Thuringia to several city-governments. Significant economic specialization and differences have developed across lands, thus promoting interterritorial competition and emulation. The variants of the German language spoken in the north and the south of the country are quite distinguishable, while at least three small language groups are legally protected within some lands.

Politically, different variants of multiparty systems have also developed in different lands permitting different formulas of multiparty coalition governments. Especially since the reunification, most land governments have been led by parties not participating in the federal government of the moment. The variety of political combinations has also produced an increasing variety of institutional and electoral system formulas among the different lands. In recent times, some observers have postulated that the lands are increasingly following the "Sinatra doctrine:" I do it my way.

The land governments form the federal upper chamber (Bundesrat), which is both the guardian of the lands' powers and the main institutional setting for cooperation among the land governments in federal policy making. The upper chamber has powers equal to those of the lower chamber regarding constitutional amendments, some suspensory veto rights over federal legislation in general, and absolute veto on legislation affecting land interests. Initially the upper chamber could veto decisions on the territory of the lands, some taxes and finances, and the creation of new federal administrative agencies within the legal domains of the lands. Yet in practice the upper chamber, representing the lands, has achieved powers equal to those of the lower chamber on most issues, thanks in part to the support given by the constitutional court. By the mid twentieth century, only ten percent of all federal laws required approval by the upper chamber. But by the early twenty-first century this proportion had increased to about 60 percent. The upper chamber also has extensive control over the federal administration, including over the implementation of federal legislation by the ministries.

The land governments do not only form the upper chamber; the latter also appoints half the members of the constitutional court as well as those of other federal organs, such as those regulating public radio and television and administering public companies. More directly, the land governments appoint half the members of the federal supreme courts (including those of civil and criminal justice, administrative contentions, and the fiscal, labor, and social courts); they also appoint half the members of the council that elects the president of the republic; as well as a majority of the council members of the central bank, which in turn is a guarantee of its independence from the federal government.

Most lands have ministries of European and international affairs; they participate in the Council of Ministers of the EU and maintain powerful embassies in Brussels and other places.

Asymmetric federations

Approaching somehow the model of federal Germany, although with a diversity of processes and institutional formulas, the larger European states are increasingly decentralized. Small political units tend to develop institutional and political formulas which are heteromorphic compared to those of the corresponding state; they create increasing asymmetries in the distribution of powers and institutional structures; and a few regions – whether called states, lands, nations, regions or autonomous communities – emerge as particularly creative and distinctive among the other units. In Europe, federalism and decentralization do not imply homogenization, but diversification. A brief survey of federalizing and regional formulas developed within European states will show this territorial diversity.

In the Belgian state, a number of successive constitutional reforms since 1970 have established increasingly decentralized federal relations. Three regions elect a parliamentary council and government, each with broad, extensive powers and unique differences: Flanders, Wallonia and Brussels. Flanders is at the same time a region and a cultural community, while Wallonia and Brussels form the French cultural community, also with its own elected institutions, and another non-regional cultural German community also exists. This framework reduces the perils of confrontation between two closed blocs. But the Dutch-speaking Flanders has asserted its own powers ahead of the French-speaking areas, which has produced a very high degree of actual self-government not yet settled in a stable formula.

In the Italian state, the traditional communes, originating in the Middle Ages, and the new metropolitan cities coexist with "special" and "ordinary" regions, but the latter are also increasingly "special." Initially, five special regions were organized with their own governmental institutions: the island of Sicily, which established its own statute immediately after the end of the Second World War in 1946, even before the Italian state adopted a democratic constitution; and four other island or bordering territories with their own languages: Sardinia and Val d'Aosta, both in 1948, Friuli–Venezia Giulia in 1963 and Trentino–Alto Adige (or South Tyrol) in 1972. Fifteen further "ordinary" regions with common regulations have been established since the 1970s. But in recent developments accompanying democratic renewal, all regions have introduced increasingly differentiated structures. While the Italian state is organized as a parliamentary regime, the regions have systems of division of powers based on separate elections for the parliament and the regional presidency. Since 2001 each region is allowed to elaborate its own statute, including the most basic institutional arrangements and the electoral system. Led by Friuli, several regions have begun to introduce significant innovations straying from the "ordinary" common rules of the past.

In the French state, the traditional communes of medieval origin and those departments historically created by the republicans were joined by democratically elected regional councils in 1986. There are 26 regions, but Corsica and four overseas departments use specific institutional formulas. Aside from these, New Caledonia has also been electing a democratic congress since 1988. While the French Fifth Republic is organized as a semi-presidential regime with separate elections for the assembly and the presidency, both based on majority rule, the regional councils are organized into a parliamentary formula based on a mixed electoral system including rules of proportional representation. This has permitted the development of different forms of political pluralism across the territory, including the formation of many regional multiparty coalitions different from those formed in the national assembly or in support of the president of the republic.

In the Austrian state, there have been nine lands with constitutions, elected parliaments and governments since the aftermath of the Second World War. Most of them hold elections by proportional representation, but with varied formulas and calendars. Although Austria is officially a federal country, its degree of decentralization is lower than that of Germany and other

European states. Actually, federal legislation prevails over land legislation on many issues. But the land governors execute not only the state's own laws, but also the federal legislation, so in this way they have been able to block several important projects enacted by the federal government. In spite of the prevalence of the German language, seven minority languages are legally protected. In some lands, citizens have a stronger identification with the land than with Austria.

Even in Britain, a recent process of "devolution" of powers to the population of traditional kingdoms and differentiated territories has developed. Northern Ireland had already elected its own House of Commons immediately after the creation of the separate Republic of Ireland in 1921. But internal division between Irish Catholics and Anglo-Unionists led to violent conflict, the suspension of autonomous institutions and a series of failed attempts at establishing a new government in the 1970s and 1980s. By 1999, however, a new Northern Ireland assembly and government were established, through the cooperation of the governments of the United Kingdom and the Republic of Ireland in actually ceding their state sovereignty. In parallel the Scottish Parliament and government and the Welsh Assembly and government were created, each with special formulas regarding legal powers and internal organization. In the three territories, different forms of proportional representation are used, in contrast to the electoral system based on single-member districts by plurality rule used for the British House of Commons; Northern Ireland has its own multiparty system; in both Scotland and Wales innovative coalition governments of laborites and liberals, as well as a Scott nationalist government, have been formed, in contrast to the tradition of single-party British cabinets.

Other instances of the territorial decentralization of traditional states include, of course, the Spanish state, which has also produced increasing differentiation among autonomous communities, as will be analyzed in the following chapter. But even some of the smaller and unitary European states, including Greece, Ireland and Portugal, have created regional entities, under the incentives provided by the EU structural and regional policy, with the aim of implementing the corresponding funds. In general, no policy area is more centralized at the state level now than it was 50 years ago, nor is there a single country in which regional governance has become weaker over the same period.

Among the more recent members of the EU in Central and Eastern Europe, there have also been important changes in the territorial distribution of power, although no formal federal formulas have been adopted. In the past there were a number of experiences of federations that failed, typically because one large unit could develop the ambition to dominate over the others. Prominent cases include Poland–Lithuania, Austria–Hungary, Czecho–Slovakia, Serbia–Croatia–Slovenia (temporarily known as Yugoslavia) and, of course, the domination of the Russian empire over Byelorussia, Estonia, Latvia, Lithuania, Moldova, Ukraine and other republics. All these federations failed because the larger unit, mentioned in the first position in each case, tried to rule over the others and the smaller units eventually chose to split. Nowadays, in contrast, most of the nations mentioned are in a position to cooperate, or may have opportunities to cooperate in the future under the much larger umbrella of the European Union, where every unit is sufficiently small, in relative terms, to avoid the possibility or temptation of one nation dominating the others.

Borderless cooperation

Transnational cooperation develops not only among regions within traditional large states, but also across state borders, leading to the formation of euro-regions and leagues of non-neighboring cities and regions. Bordering regions encompass 46 percent of the European territory and 32 percent of the European population. As borders, customs, police controls and currency exchange offices have vanished, neighboring regions located on either side of former frontiers tend to coordinate their common interests and develop "good practice" solutions. Relevant areas of cooperation include rural and agricultural development, transport, bridges, environment, media, education, and tourism. Close relations are facilitated by language and religious proximity, the existence of well-established and active local government structures and the identification of specific common purposes.

Regional transfrontier cooperation has been supported by the European Commission through a succession of programs such as the multiannual "Interreg" from 1989 on, as well as by the European Parliament, which has formally "encouraged transfrontier cooperation at all levels." In contrast, certain state central governments have shown themselves reluctant to lose control over their peripheral territories.

Initial experiences of regional transfrontier cooperation developed since the late 1950s, especially with the Euregio created in Gronau, around the border between Germany and the Netherlands, later expanded towards Belgium. In parallel, several councils were formed in Scandinavia, including those of Oresund, North Carlotte and Kvarken, around the state borders of Denmark, Finland, Norway and Sweden. The Association of European Border Regions, created in 1971, includes about 90 members.

Currently, there exist 61 euro-regions, which have developed more than 150 programs based on bilateral or trilateral agreements and treaties for cross-border cooperation since the 1980s. The euro-regions are mostly located in: the Benelux area, that is, around the borders between Belgium, the Netherlands and Luxembourg; in Central Europe, especially across the German borders with Austria, the Czech republic and Poland; and in Scandinavia, especially across the borders of Finland, Sweden and Norway (the latter not formally belonging to the EU).

Cases in which multiregional cooperation has produced a public law administrative structure include the Euregio Ems-Dollart, formed by the

Dutch provinces of Groningen and Drenthe and the German territories of Ostfriesland, Emsland, and the Cloppenburg district, as well as the Euregio Rhine–Waal, formed between the Netherlands and Germany with the German lands Northern Rhine–Westphalia, Lower Saxony and an association of municipalities. Other interesting cases include, for example, the Baltic euro-region, formed by Bornholm in Denmark, Klaipeda in Lithuania, Kurzeme in Latvia, Warmia-Masurian in Poland, Kronoberg in Sweden, and the Russian enclave of Kaliningrad that is encircled by EU territory. Likewise, the euro-region Pomerania covers the first new frontier drawn between Sweden and Brandenburg after the Westphalia Treaty and that between Germany and Poland – a very "hot" one through the two World Wars and the Cold War. The Pomeranian region is formed by several local authorities in the German lands of Mecklenburg–Western Pomerania and Brandenburg, the Southern Swedish region of Scania and the Polish province of Zachodniopomorskie, where the Polish city of Szczecin might regain its historical position as a communications crossroads, as well as its role as a seaport for Berlin.

A couple of examples can also illustrate how interstate borders have been vanishing across Europe. The Euregio and the Ems-Dollart region, mentioned above, developed the project of the motorway A31-Emsland with cross-border funds. This route connects the Ruhr Basin and the North Sea coast through territories in the German lands of North Rhine–Westphalia and Lower Saxony; it also connects with the Amsterdam–Berlin motorway and can be easily accessed from the Netherlands, but in fact is entirely grounded on German territory. When the German federal government dropped the plans for the motorway, the euro-regions mentioned above mobilized private and EU resources, and contributed to financing the project, built entirely within German territory, with Dutch taxpayer funds.

The first transfrontier hospital in Europe is being built in Puigcerdà, within Spanish state territory, thanks to an agreement between the governments of the euro-region formed by Catalonia, Aragon and the Balearic Islands on one side of the border, and Languedoc–Roussillon and Midi-Pyrennées on the other. The hospital location is in la Cerdanya, a historical valley and a county artfully divided since the seventeenth century between the French and the Spanish states that even manages to include a Spanish enclave encircled by French territory, the town of Llívia. French citizens from several towns used to attend the old hospital located on the Spanish side of the border, but the hospital administrators and authorities claimed the corresponding payments, until they made the agreement to build a new common service.

Borderless cooperation has also developed between non-neighboring cities and regions across Europe. Interesting experiences include the Conference of Peripheral and Maritime Regions of Europe, as well as Eurocities, a grouping of the largest cities in the continent. More specifically, the New Hanse is a league of cities and towns that had belonged in the late medieval past to the Hanseatic League of merchants that expanded from North German territories into an area presently covered by seven states. Currently, cities like Lubeck in Germany, Zwolle in the Netherlands, Gdansk in Poland and Bruges in Belgium form the skeleton of a new Hanseatic network grouping about 100 cities and towns. Similarly, a league called 4 Motors for Europe is formed by four relatively developed regions within their respective states, Baden–Wurttemberg in Germany, Rhone–Alps in France, Lombardy in Italy, and Catalonia in Spain. They cooperate on issues of culture, education, economy and territorial planning while aspiring to contribute to the building of the EU with a regionalizing perspective.

All in all, traditional interstate direct relations and cooperation, based on a mutual recognition of sovereignty, is increasingly being replaced within the European Union by direct relations among small units formally organized as states, regions, cities, or other structures. Cross-border cooperation between regional and local governments eliminates a crucial element of state sovereignty. It also breaks the concentric structure of cities, regions, states and the EU by introducing transversal relations and institutions. Small units within a large empire are eroding the central role of the states and contributing to the creation of a broad diversity of political structures and forms of self-government, though they are not yet well represented within the institutions of the EU.

11 A case of a failing nation–state

Spain is probably the clearest case of failure in the attempt to build a large nation–state in Europe. Initially, from the sixteenth century on, the building of a broad Spanish empire, which expanded through Europe, the Americas, Asia and Africa, helped to create collaborative links among the several traditional kingdoms existing on the Iberian Peninsula. Especially important was Castile–Leon's initiative towards Aragon–Catalonia, Navarre and Portugal. But the more modern attempt to build a unitary Spanish state and a Spanish nation under Castilian domination, from the eighteenth century on, clashed with resistance from several national groups and was fatally blunted by the weakness of the Spanish empire.

As Spain, which had once been a great imperial power, tried in the nineteenth century to affirm its sovereignty vis-à-vis the other large states, it was defeated first by Great Britain and then by France, and lost most of its colonies. In the twentieth century, it was left out of the two World Wars and, after the Second World War, as a dictatorship, it was initially excluded from the United Nations Organization, the NATO and the European Community. The imperial defeat weakened the state, which was unable to integrate "nationally" the inhabitants of the Iberian Peninsula.

From extinguished empire to failed state

At the beginning of the modern era, the population of the three old kingdoms of the Crown of Aragon where the Catalan language was spoken (Aragon, Catalonia and Valencia) was three times less than that of Castile, a proportion fostering Castilian temptation to impose its domination. The small nation of Portugal, open to the Atlantic, was able to escape from that domination by relying upon its own transcontinental empire, but Catalonia, locked onto the Mediterranean Sea, could project only towards the Iberian peninsula. For a couple of centuries, however, the relations between the kingdom of Castile and those of Aragon, Catalonia and Valencia basically amounted to a confederation. The expansion of the Castilian language from the sixteenth century on, for instance, was promoted as a replacement for

Latin as a new lingua franca for written communication, but not necessarily at the expense of Catalan or any other of the languages spoken in the diverse traditional communities.

The attempt to building a Spanish state emerged more clearly during the eighteenth century. After the Westphalia treaty blessed the large states' sovereignty in Europe, the Bourbons' new monarchy tried to copy the centralized model of the French state for the Iberian Peninsula. The "New Plan" model established by the Bourbons implied a uniform control of all peninsular territories from Madrid, which was organized analogously to the administration of the overseas colonies, that is, around a captain–general and a royal audience in each territory. During the eighteenth century, there was an intensification of forced military recruits and the imposition of the Castilian language (to the point of suppressing almost all Catalan universities, for example).

The Catalans and the Basques, though they were deprived of their own self-government, could access broader markets more easily thanks to the suppression of customs between the old kingdoms in the peninsula and the establishment of a unified external commerce tariff. The exchanges with the colonies also increased the links among the population. The opening of broad markets resumed during the nineteenth century, thanks to the securities provided by new civil, criminal and commercial codes, the defense of property, the adoption of the decimal metric system and the creation of the peseta, all occurring in parallel to the closing of the Spanish trade market through the prohibition of agricultural imports and other protections for Spanish producers.

All these developments tended toward building a Spanish nation, prosperous and modern, on the basis of an efficient Spanish state and an imperial ambition. But they did not imply culturally uniform patterns. The Catalans, in particular, continued to see the Castilian language as an imperial lingua franca permitting communication with the Spaniards and the colonies, rather than as a single, national and exclusive language. Castilian was not actually imposed as the single language in schools until 1888 and was not declared the "official language" until 1931, a very late date suggesting a rather defensive reaction to its failure as a national language.

The crucial crisis was the fall of the remnants of the Spanish empire in 1898 as a consequence of military defeat by the United States and the independence of Cuba, Puerto Rico and the Philippines. The importance of this moment did not derive from the size of the colonies lost, since far more land had been lost during the first half of the nineteenth century in North and South America, but particularly from the feeling that, with this defeat, Spain would be isolated from the rest of the world. By the late nineteenth century broad new international economic relations were developing, thanks to new advances in communication and transport, as has been analyzed in a previous chapter of this book. While Great Britain consolidated itself as the first world power, the Spanish defeat in the Caribbean and the Pacific was caused by a new emerging power, the United States of America, which was then culminating its own territorial expansion and empire building. In the aftermath of the 1898 defeat, probably many thought that the conservative leader Antonio Cánovas del Castillo had been right when he said that "Spaniards are those who cannot be anything else." An entire generation of literary writers, philosophers and historians, known as the "98 generation," was lost in an agonizing meditation on the essence of Spain. From this moment forward, many Spaniards developed low levels of national self-esteem.

In Catalonia and the Basque country, the disappearance of the Spanish empire weakened popular support for the project of building a Spanish state and a Spanish nation, which ceased to look sufficiently appealing. For the entrepreneurial Catalans who had tried to lead the modernization of Spain, this was also a defeat, for which they sought consolation through a movement of internal affirmation. From that moment on, many Catalans and Basques, each group on its own, tried to be "something else," to paraphrase Cánovas.

In Catalonia in particular, as alternatives to the failed projects of a Spanish nation and a Spanish state, there was not only the search for a new Catalan nation and a new Catalan state designed to more or less federalize a larger area, but also the dream of a new Catalan empire as a replacement for the extinguished Spanish empire. The political movement known as "Catalanism" was conceived of from the beginning as an instrument for the creation of a "Great Spain," which may have included Portugal; there was great admiration for the United States; also the model of the dual and asymmetric empire of Austria–Hungary was frequently used; in general, there was an explicit wish to build a "Greater Catalonia" of an imperial type. Francesc Cambó, leader of the Catalan regionalists, was accused by Spanish unionists of trying to be "at the same time Bolívar of Catalonia and Bismarck of Spain," that is, the leader of the independence (from Spain) and the driver of a great empire (like the German one). But the two aims were not and are not contradictory; they have been the two essential and inseparable aims not only of the Catalanist movement at the beginning of the twentieth century. As has been sketched above, they were characteristic of all main Catalan political movements for several centuries: Catalonia's self-government and the participation of self-governed Catalonia in an area of imperial size – "liberty and empire," as it was put by the greatest Catalan and Spanish historian of the twentieth century, Jaume Vicens-Vives. Also during the late period of the twentieth century, Catalan political movements gave enthusiastic support to the project of building a united Europe. As was stated by a Spanish philosopher, speaking for many, "Spain was the problem and Europe, the solution."

The Spanish state is not what it was

After a very long period of extreme political and institutional instability and several dictatorships, during the last quarter of the twentieth century a new democratic regime was established in Spain, initially with broad social and political support. The building of democracy, however, led to integration in the European empire, which has weakened enormously the foundations of the Spanish state. With democracy, the nations of Catalonia and Euskadi (or the Basque country), as well as other territories in the peninsula, have also developed increasing demands for self-government. These demands have been fostered by new access to large-scale public goods provided by the European Union (which make the Spain-wide state less necessary), competition between territorial autonomous governments for redistributing resources accumulated by the Spanish state, and the democratic advantages that small nations gain by having their own institutions.

First, the Spanish army, partly integrated into NATO structures since 1981, is nowadays a small and ineffective body. Military expenditure, which had been above two percent of GDP in 1990, at the peak of the Cold War, has been reduced to less than one percent. The compulsory draft, which had been a traumatic experience for millions of young Spaniards since the late nineteenth century, was shortened in duration at the end of the 1980s, but an avalanche of conscientious objectors and desertions moved the government to accelerate plans for its elimination. Initially, it was officially projected that the number of military personnel, which was 375,000 when Spain joined NATO, would be reduced to 120,000 professionals, but in fact, for lack of volunteers, the number of troops has been reduced to less than 70,000 of which only 7,000 are permanent. About ten percent of the soldiers and marines have been recruited in foreign countries, especially in Latin America. The mix of professional mercenaries, temporary soldiers and foreign recruits implies a return to pre-state formulas from before the nineteenth century.

The National Defense Directive of 2004, which should orient Spanish military policy for the coming years, does not, in contrast to similar directives in previous periods, refer to the aims of guaranteeing the sovereignty and independence of Spain, its territorial integrity or the constitutional order. Territorial defense has actually been replaced by a security objective shared with the allied states, especially within NATO. But the Spanish government wants to make any participation in an external action conditional on a multilateral mandate and the active decision of the Spanish Parliament, which implies in practice general abstention.

Second, the Spanish state has also ceased to be sovereign in monetary and commercial policies, due to the adoption of the euro and the European common market, and is subject to serious restrictions on budget and fiscal policies by the European stability plans. Foreign trade amounts to up to 60 percent of the Spanish GDP, three-fourths of which comes from countries of the EU. As has been discussed in other chapters of this book, supranational integration induces higher regional specialization and differentiation. Regional differences in per capita income throughout Spain have been compensated in part by redistribution of public funds, both Spanish and European, but it seems that most of them have been spent in consumption rather than investment and, although they have produced increases in disposable income, have not fostered big improvements in the receiving regions' productive performance. It is clearer than ever that the Spanish regions which, before redistribution, attain higher levels of income per capita than the state average are those that are closer to the center of Europe, that is, those located along the traditional border with France; the Basque country, Navarre, La Rioja, Aragon, Catalonia and the Balearic Islands, to which the overprotected Madrid is added. The control of the center over the periphery thus decreases not only in political and administrative terms, but also economically, to which the central government tries to react with territorial redistribution.

Third, homogenization of language and culture in Spain not only did not culminate in a nation–state of the French type, but has decreased during recent decades. Around one-fourth of Spaniards use a language different from Castilian as the main language in their family and private relations and about 40 percent live in the six territorially autonomous communities in which there are two official languages. The multilingualism of Spanish state citizens includes not only Castilian, Catalan, Galician and Basque, but also Asturian, Aragonese, Arabic, Occitan and Portuguese.

The Spanish state is, therefore, not what it was, and neither will it be what it could have been, a uniform nation–state under the Westphalian and French models. It actually tends to move increasingly away from that model. Certainly, public expenditure has increased very much during the present democratic period. In 1975, at the end of the dictatorship, the state spent little more than 20 percent of GDP, while thirty years later it has more than doubled that percentage. As GDP in real terms (discounting inflation) has also doubled in these thirty years, it turns out that public expenditure in real terms has multiplied by more than four. But whereas in 1975 the central administration spent 90 percent of all public expenditure (and only 10 percent was in the hands of municipalities), nowadays the central expenditure is hardly 50 percent of the total (and the largest part is spent on social security and debt interest). As a proportion of GDP, the central administration expenditure is, thus, about the same or even lower than thirty years ago, whilst the main novelty is that a new and extensive administration of the territorially autonomous communities has been built.

In terms of public employees, the degree of decentralization is even greater, since the autonomous communities exert powers in service activities employing many people, such as in education and health care. So while the proportion of public employees in the central administration relative to the total employed population is nowadays lower than thirty years ago, a numerous autonomous administration has been created. Given the decrease in soldiers and marines mentioned above, as well as the decentralization of police and security forces, it turns out that the central administration has consolidated its highest proportion of civil servants in finance, that is, in personnel directly or indirectly involved in collecting taxes.

Centrifugal autonomies

The so-called Spanish "state of autonomies" has generated steady competition between territorial autonomous communities in obtaining a redistribution of public resources. Territorial differences have been maintained and increased. There have been frequent revisions of institutional rules, the division of powers and financial criteria. The "autonomic state" is not, therefore, an equilibrium, in the sense of a stable institutional solution for the relations between different territorial communities, but a frame for competition among territories and for the development of increasing demands for self-government.

During the transition to democracy, all anti-Franco and pro-democracy groups proposed the establishment of institutions for the self-government of Catalonia, the Basque country and Galicia – three nations with remote historical precedents, who have approved their autonomy during the previous Second Republic and who speak their own languages, none of which is Castilian. During the negotiation of a new constitution in the late 1970s there was a convergence between four strategies: the self-government programs of the Catalan, Basque and Galician nationalisms; some expanded demands through several provinces and regions in imitation of the former; the subsequent position of the government party, the Union of Democratic Center (UCD), to give "coffee for all" or prepare a "table of cheeses" (as was said at the time); and the federalist tradition of part of the Spanish left. Up to 17 "autonomous" territorial governments were thus formed, in most cases without historical precedents.

The framework initially established in the Spanish constitution in 1978 implied a distinction between the three autonomous communities with precedents of democratic self-government and particular languages – Catalonia, the Basque country and Galicia – which would have special regimes, and the others, for which a common regime was provided. But the differences among communities have been increasingly complex. First, the Basque country regained its historical privileges *("fueros")* as the basis for a special formula of finances, permitting the autonomous collection of all taxes and the enactment of other particular institutions. Navarre did the same, but not Catalonia or Galicia. Andalusia adopted from the beginning the model of division of powers that was initially reserved for only the three "historic" communities. As a consequence of entry into the European Community, the Canary Islands acceded to special fiscal formulas to compensate for their distance from Spain. Later on, the autonomous cities of Ceuta and Melilla, also in Africa, were also granted special regimes. Specific language differences, or the condition of being an island, have necessitated other formulas.

An average of eight of the 17 autonomic presidents have not belonged to the party of the prime minister of the central government, which has alternated between the center-left Socialist party and the conservative People's party (which replaced the UCD on the right side of the political spectrum). In particular, since 1980, Catalonia, the Basque country, and the Canary Islands have been governed by local nationalist parties almost without interruption. On several occasions, the Catalan nationalist parties Convergence and Union (CiU) and the Republican Left of Catalonia (ERC), as well as the Basque Nationalist Party (PNV) and the Canary Coalition (CC), have been pivotal in the formation of a legislative majority in the Spanish parliament by whichever Spain-wide party is in power. In exchange, the nationalist parties in their communities have asked for more powers and financial resources, thus fostering a permanent decentralization of the state.

The degree of competition among the different autonomous communities has also been high because the institutional framework of the state has weak mechanisms for multilateral negotiation and cooperation. In contrast to the usual situation in federal states, the Spanish Senate does not represent territories and tends to have a party composition very similar to that of the lower chamber, the Congress of Deputies, or even one more favorable to the two larger Spain-wide parties. The autonomous communities do not participate formally in the appointment of bodies that are designed to guarantee the division of powers, especially the Constitutional Tribunal, the General Council of the Judicial Power, the board of the national bank or the board of public radio and television. In contrast to typical large federal states, there is not a council of autonomic presidents or of regular meetings between these presidents and the prime minister. The sectorial conferences by members of autonomic governments tend to be the setting for negotiating new transfers of power to them rather than a coordinating body for Spain-wide public policy.

As a consequence of competitive demands from territorial governments, successive fiscal agreements have been made to increase the amount of resources in the hands of the autonomous communities, which have triggered new demands. From 1987 on, the government of Catalonia began to organize its own police force on the model of the Basque police, which has replaced the national police and the civil guard in most cases. The Canary Islands, Navarre and Valencia obtained powers over health care beyond those included in their initial statutes of autonomy. During the 1990s, all communities obtained powers over education. From 2004 on, most communities of the Spanish state began to discuss new statutes of autonomy, following the initiative of Euskadi and Catalonia. In all cases the autonomous communities intend to enlarge their self-governing capacity, while some autonomic leaders have explicitly stated their objective of obtaining powers at least as broad as those of the Catalans.

In parallel to this process of thinning the Spanish state, the sense of belonging to a Spanish nation have also been increasingly weakened. Less than one-fourth of the citizens of the Spanish state consider themselves to be only or mainly Spaniards (rather than from their autonomous community). Less than ten percent would prefer to go back to a unitary state, while among the rest, almost half think that the current degree of decentralization of the "state of autonomies" is insufficient.

All of this confirms that, in the twenty-first century, building a Spanish nation–state, in the sense of a political organization based on effective sovereignty, power monopoly and the homogenization of the population, is a nonviable endeavor. The Spanish state has not only sacrificed its capacity to guarantee the defense of the territory and provide a currency and a protected market to NATO, the EU and other organizations of imperial size. It has also lost a large part of its capacity to collect taxes, maintain order and security for its citizens, create public works programs and organize basic services such as education and health care, in favor of autonomous communities. Against old expectations, the establishment of democracy in Spain has not helped to build a large nation–state. Rather, it has favored the integration of Spain into a very large empire along with the development of small, increasingly self-governing nations.

12 Multilevel democracy

In contrast to empires of the past, building Europe-wide common institutions has required consensus among its member states on democratic principles. The principle of democratic government and the development of market-oriented economic relations have been the flagships for the process of building the European Union. While every candidate to become a member of the EU has to fulfill strict conditions of freedom and democracy, these also guide the hand of Europe-wide institutional design.

Through half a century, Europe-wide political institutions have evolved from those corresponding to an international organization based on diplomatic relations to others approaching a federal union. During the initial period, the central institution was the Council of Ministers, which was formed by representatives of the governments of the member states, as in any regular international organization. Influential leaders at the time included the French Jean Monnet, the German Konrad Adenauer and the Italian Alcide de Gasperi. As each member state considered itself to be sovereign, it had the power of veto on collective decisions, which means that most decisions were made unanimously. In point of fact, many important strategic decisions were made at summit meetings of heads of government, a practice institutionalized as the European Council.

This traditionally diplomatic, interstate or intergovernmental model of decision making eventually proved highly ineffective, since a single member state's veto was able to paralyze any collective initiative. In reaction, a number of decisions began to be enforced by only a subset of the member states, giving way to what has been called "reinforced," "closer" or "enhanced" cooperation, as well as "variable geometry," "concentric circles," "strong core," "two speeds," "à la carte," "flexible" and other metaphors. Decisions made in this manner include the Social Chapter (excluding Britain), the Security Information Service or Schengen agreement on police and border control (including 12 members and four non-members of the EU) and the common currency, the euro (which is accepted by only 13 member states but is increasingly used elsewhere, as mentioned before). With these decisions, most of the larger states of Europe ceased to be able to exert "sovereignty" on matters that had defined their fundamental powers since the seventeenth century or so: army, police, borders, customs, and currency. The diversity of units included in the different common matters was also typically "imperial."

Further institutional developments fostered more federal-oriented relations, especially since the presidency of the European Commission by Jacques Delors. They include, in particular, joint decision making by a qualified majority of the Council of Ministers and the simple majority of the European Parliament, with the aim of being implemented in all the countries of the EU. With these procedures, the territorial units, as represented in the Council, share decision making power with parliamentary representatives of the European people at large.

However, the two processes of external expansion and internal institutionalization of the EU have not always matched well. The process of enlargement was accelerated: the first enlargement from six to nine members took almost 20 years; further enlargements of three members each were then approved after successive lapses of about ten years each; but on the latest occasion no less than 12 new members joined. In parallel, institutional instability was also increasing. The founding Treaty of Rome was modified only after almost 30 years by the Single European Act; but from that moment on, a series of treaties were approved within increasingly shorter periods: Maastricht, Amsterdam, Nice, the latter almost immediately replaced by an attempt at a so-called Constitution, which finally failed. Putting an end to the long process of unlimited territorial expansion appeared then as a necessary condition for the EU to achieve internal institutional stability.

An interesting analogy can be drawn to the process of building the empire of the United States of America during the nineteenth century, which also involved a gradual expansion (in that case from the 13 initial member states to the present 50) introducing territorial tensions and a very lethal civil war between formerly independent states. Finally, the limits of the American Union, which are not fixed in the US constitution, were established in fact in the Caribbean Sea, where several new candidates to join were discarded in spite of having belonged to the same empire (the Spanish) as other members that had already been incorporated. For instance, California was split into two units, one inside and the other outside the Union; Puerto Rico was associated to the Union, but the closer Cuba was not. The Caribbean became then the USA's "backyard," that is, a conflictive and politically unstable zone whence there has been a ceaseless flow of migrants.

But only when those external limits were fixed, at the beginning of the twentieth century and several decades after the civil war, was the USA able to complete the institutionalization of internal federal relations between the union and a variety of state and local governments. Meanwhile, the USA remained in relative isolation from the rest of the world, lacking a consistent foreign policy beyond its own continent, in spite of the huge development of international transport, communications and trade during that period.

Analogously to the American experience, the construction of the EU empire has required a gradual enlargement of its territory during the several decades after the very lethal Second World War – which was also a civil war across European states – until today when more or less fixed territorial limits are being established. By discarding several new candidates to join, the EU risks relegating the remaining Balkan states, and other republics that have historically belonged to the same empire as accepted members, to a "backyard" out of which may arise conflict, instability and a permanent flow of immigrants. For instance, Slovenia has become a member state of the Union, but Serbia and others of its former partners in Yugoslavia remain outside; the Baltic republics joined the EU, but other former Soviet republics did not.

Only under conditions of a stable membership and territorial stability, however, may the EU be able to design a relatively durable internal institutional framework. When this is achieved, the EU might even be able to develop a consistent foreign policy beyond its own continent.

European political parties

Recent important changes in inter-institutional relations that have eroded the sovereignty of the member states within the EU have been in large part the result of initiatives by political parties, rather than by the governments of states. Political parties in the European Parliament have been involved in a long process of forming increasingly large European political groups, which has enhanced the Parliament's ability to make collective decisions; this has then facilitated interinstitutional cooperation, and made the governance of the highly pluralistic EU relatively effective and consensual.

Paralleling successive enlargements of the EU, increasing numbers of different political parties running independently in elections have obtained representation in the European Parliament – from about 40 in the first direct election in 1979 up to more than 120 in 2004. But the increase in the number of electoral parties obtaining seats has not caused a growth in the total number of political groups within the Parliament. On the contrary, the degree of concentration of deputies in a few large groups has increased steadily since 1979, and the absolute number of European political groups has decreased after the most recent elections (from 11 in 1989 to only eight after the 2004 election).

The formation of increasingly large, aggregative Europe-wide political groups in the European Parliament during the late twentieth and early twenty-first centuries can be compared to certain processes of forming increasingly large, aggregative statewide political parties in the state parliaments of European countries during the late nineteenth and early twentieth centuries (as, for instance, in Britain, France, Germany and Spain). Many political representatives of the time were strongly rooted in local constituencies and promoted local interests with no clear priorities on broad issues, while holding vague ideological positions.

The aggregation of local representatives into statewide parties created more uniform policies and greater ideological homogeneity among political representatives while contributing to a reinforcement of the role of parliaments, much the same as the aggregation of representatives in European political groups is now promoting more effective decision making and contributing to the institutional strength of the European Parliament. To the extent that many political parties are subject to majority decisions within a few large European political groups and to the corresponding group's voting discipline in the Parliament, nationalistic positions against an ever-closer union of Europe have less prominence in the institutional process.

The aggregative effort has developed asymmetrically, but continuously across the spectrum from left to right. On the center-left, the European Socialist Party, which was very large from the beginning, was further enlarged by the Italian post-communists and others, uniting up to 20 parties. Previously, the European Communist Group had been dominated by the Italian communists, the largest leftist party in Italy at the time. Yet the Communist Group became decreasingly powerful within the European Parliament, while the Italians, who transformed themselves into the Party of Democratic Left, entered the European Socialist Party.

On the center-right, the European People's Party initially gathered together christian–democratic parties from nine countries. But it gradually integrated other parties from countries without strong traditions of christian-democracy, including the conservatives from Britain, Denmark and Spain, as well as members of other small European groups led by the French Gaullists and Forza Italia, among others.

Some observers have noted that the degree of internal ideological homogeneity of the European People's Party has been somewhat diminished by the successive integration of new parties, with some tensions developing between christian-democrats and more conservative partners. But it is dubious that, for instance, the British conservatives, the Central European christian-democrats, the French Gaullists and Forza Italia, in different European Political Groups for some time but later integrated into the European People's Party, were much less close to each other than, say, the British laborites, the Central European and Nordic social-democrats, the Mediterranean socialists and the Italian post-communists, all united within the European Socialist Party.

A comparable process of gradual enlargement also took place among the liberals, who incorporated both liberal–conservative and liberal–radical parties. These different orientations can be distinguished between parties in different countries, but they also exist in the form of two separate parties in some countries such as Belgium and the Netherlands. Accordingly, the European gathering adopted the pluralistic name of Liberal, Democratic and Reform Group. More recently, the Catalan and the Basque nationalists have also joined this Group.

In spite of their increasingly large recruitment, internal cohesion of the European political groups has improved steadily through successive legislative periods. The average proportions of individual members of the Parliament voting in accordance with their European Political Group have risen over time: from 74 percent in 1984–1989 to 90 percent in 1999–2000, as shown by calculations based on roll call votes. The largest groups, the populars, the socialists, and the liberals, as well as the greens, have reached the highest degrees of discipline in voting, between 90 and 95 percent. Internal cohesion of European political groups in the European Parliament is certainly not lower than that of political parties in the US Congress.

The rationale behind all this increasing aggregation of a huge variety of political and territorial representation is that each party can expect to have more global influence within the European Parliament by being a member of a large, powerful European political group. In spite of representing the citizens of a high number of countries with their own political regimes and party systems, the European Parliament has a higher level of aggregation and a lower number of large parties than the parliaments of several European countries, such as Belgium, Denmark, Finland and the Netherlands.

The basic ideological affinities between the European political groups tend to be located on the left–right axis, as in most state parliaments. "Moderate" parties tend to prevail. The party configuration based on the socialists on the center-left, the liberals at the center, and the christians on the center-right, with other minor parties on both sides, closely resembles the domestic party structure in Germany, and it is not very dissimilar to the distribution of parties in Belgium, the Netherlands and Luxembourg. In all European elections, the socialists, the populars and the liberals together have gathered more than 70 percent of the total seats. Hence, a supermajority centrist coalition could always be formed with these three groups.

Europe-wide parties and multiparty parliamentary coalitions create intermediate aggregation mechanisms between highly pluralistic political and territorial representation and European-level decision making. In this way, the European Parliament has been able to become an active partner in the interinstitutional process and to create federalizing links with the other institutions. In other words, political party strategies fill the gap that is left by loose institutional regulations and constraints, as well as by the reluctance of states to cede power, and make EU interinstitutional relations relatively tight and effective.

Governance in the making

In order to make the unity and the diversity of the EU compatible through democratic governance, a number of requirements not entirely fulfilled by the most recent regulations must be met. The EU cannot try to replicate the institutional mechanisms that were characteristic of its member states in their ambition to establish sovereign and homogeneous rule over a well-defined territory. A better model of democratic governance lies at the core of Europe, encircled by but remaining outside the EU: the Helvetic Confederation or Switzerland.

Like the EU, the current institutional configuration of Switzerland resulted from a very long history of interrelations among very old republics and other previously existing political units. Initially only three units (cantons) formed a league, which gradually expanded up to the present 23 units. Like in much larger units, the Swiss population has maintained and developed a variety of languages, territorial forms of organization and religious allegiances. The confederal government is based on powers limited to defense, trade and legal matters, while all other powers are in the hands of the cantonal governments. At the confederal level, there is a two-chamber parliament, in which the upper chamber represents the territories on an egalitarian basis and the lower chamber is elected by proportional representation – analogous to the way the European Council of Ministers represents the territorial units and the European Parliament is elected across Europe by proportional representation. The Swiss executive, which is formally appointed by the two chambers, is based on multiparty "grand coalition" formulas, usually encompassing more than 80 percent of the popular vote. There is also a collective presidency with a chair rotating for short periods. These formulas are analogous, respectively, to the broad composition of the European Commission and the rotating presidency of the European Council.

The compounding units of the Swiss Confederation, the cantons, are rather small and highly homogeneous in social and ethnic, language, and religious characteristics, which has facilitated the development of well-settled and broadly admired forms of democracy. They have their own constitutions, maintain extensive powers and must confirm by popular referendum most decisions made at the confederal level. Cantonal secession is permitted, as happened with the formation of the new canton of Jura splitting from Bern in 1975. There are an interesting variety of institutional formulas at the territorial level, including local direct democracy, separate elections for cantonal parliaments, governments, and, sometimes, presidents, as well as a variety of municipal and cantonal arrangements.

For the EU to approach this model of a democratic government, but at a much larger scale, it will need to improve to some degree its interinstitutional relations and overcome the so-called "democratic deficit." First, the Council of Ministers, which represents the citizens of each country through their own institutions and tends to work on the basis of each country's interests rather than on strict ideological positions, should be considered, as mentioned, an upper chamber of territorial representation. Accordingly, the Council is increasingly made up of representatives of not only the state governments, but also the substate, "regional" governments and parliaments. A further improvement could give the Council as many representatives per member state as votes, which would facilitate regular participation of regional governments.

Likewise, the European Parliament should be considered the lower chamber, the representative institution of the European citizens. A more homogeneous electoral system among the member states, resulting in more intense Europe-wide electoral campaigns, would help to produce such a representation. Both chambers, the Council and the Parliament, should develop significant legislative powers and a mutual veto. Since the Council and the Parliament are elected separately and by different rules, they tend to have different political party majorities. The corresponding interinstitutional decisions tend thus to be based on very broad agreements encompassing two different majorities.

The European Commission should be considered the EU's executive. Accordingly, the Commission, which is already appointed by the two parliamentary chambers, should also be fully accountable. Its political composition should be more consistent with the party composition of the Council and the Parliament, but it could also adopt a supermajority, "grand coalition" formula.

Even more prominently, a better arrangement of the EU institutions should give more representation and decision making power to the smaller territorial units – comparable with the way the Swiss cantons are required to consent to and can block federal initiatives. Only democratic practices at the lower territorial levels can develop citizens' participation to the point of covering the current "democratic deficit" of the EU. The officially adopted principle of "subsidiarity" indeed favors the allocation of decision making power to the smallest political unit capable of dealing effectively with the corresponding issue, but the subsequent distribution of powers is subject to case by case specifications.

As mentioned, land, regional or autonomous governments can currently participate in the Council of Ministers, an arrangement consistent with the role of territorial representation corresponding to that of the Council as the upper chamber. Since 1993, a state can be represented in the Council of Ministers by a substate minister, a regular practice for the regions of Belgium and the lands of Germany and, together with the state minister, for the lands of Austria, the nations of Britain and, more recently, the autonomous communities of Spain, particularly on matters of agriculture, industry, environment, research, education, culture, territorial planning, and tourism. In 2001, for the first time, a Council of Ministers of the EU, that of Research, was presided over by a regional minister (from Brussels-capital).

Less clearly a part of the EU institutional framework is the Committee of the Regions. The initial impulse came from the German land governments with the aim of preserving their decision making powers within the European framework. Most autonomous communities in Spain also joined the demand for more consistent territorial representation within the EU. The Assembly of European Regions and the Council of European Municipalities and

Regions, together with the Associations of Border Regions and of Peripheral Maritime Regions, acted as pressure groups for institutional recognition. Nowadays, the Committee of the Regions is only an advisory body to the European Commission on issues related to the competence of regional and local governments in the fields of transport, telecommunications, energy, public health, education and culture, as well as on the management of structural and developmental funds. Its members aspire to the right to obligatory consultation by the Commission and the right to appeal to the European Court on issues under their jurisdiction.

The governance of the EU thus implies multiple levels of institutions of which none – neither the union, nor each of the states, nor any smaller unit – can be considered to be "sovereign" any more. Legislative, executive and judicial powers may be exerted at different levels and throughout different territories. Since no "sovereign" power can exist, the difference between formulas for small units that have traditionally been called "independence" and "autonomy" is nowadays only a question of degree. But in order to protect their self-government from any centralizing power, small communities need to have a seat at the table of the EU. Sharing decision making power in the larger supranational organizations is a necessary condition for the success of small nations.

Conclusion

After sovereignties

In the previous pages we have discussed the economic and political viability in the present world of small nations like Bavaria, Catalonia, Flanders, Kashmir, Quebec, or Scotland, to mention just a few, in comparison to many small, formally independent states like Estonia, Ireland, Singapore, Slovenia, or Uruguay, again to mention just a few. Many small "independent" states and "autonomous" regions in the present world would not be viable as separate political units if they did not belong to large imperial areas of free trade, defense and communication and take benefit from the corresponding provision of large-scale public goods. But membership of vast imperial units makes a small community's broad self-government possible without its own army, borders or customs.

There are two kinds of arguments in favor of small nations' self-government, respectively related to efficiency and democracy. First, the efficient provision of public goods requires diverse territorial scales. Due to the development of transport and communication technologies, efficient scales for the provision of defense, security, communication, and market rules, which may be very large, do not necessarily correspond with those regarding local commerce, daily transport or the preservation of certain natural resources, nor with those for public education, health policy or personal services, which are better provided in small areas with homogeneous populations. In an ideal world of efficiency, each public good should be provided in an area encompassing its consumers, who should finance them. Multilevel governance with different areas of institutional jurisdiction within an "imperial"-sized territory approaches the ideal. In contrast, the traditional model of sovereign state pretended that one size fits all – and, as in the Procustean bed, those not fitting were amputated. Nowadays, the typical single-size state is too small for some goods and too large for others.

Second, democracy as a means to make collective decisions by voting and elections can work better in small communities, which tend to have relatively more homogeneous populations than large states. Small size and low heterogeneity make it relatively easy to develop public deliberation to identify common interests and priority public goods, the aggregation of citizens' preferences into acceptable collective decisions, and consensual implementation of enforceable decisions. The total number of individuals who can see their preferences satisfied by governmental decisions is higher if the population is organized in a set of many small units making their own decisions than if it does in a single, large unit.

From an efficient and democratic perspective, therefore, collective decisions should preferably be made by the smallest possible community within a set of multiple institutional levels – that is, according to the classical criterion of "subsidiarity" (which has been formally adopted, for instance, by the European Union).

All this questions the notion of sovereignty, which was an essential attribute of modern states. In contrast to traditional large empires with shared powers and overlapping jurisdictions, a state concentrates power around a territorial center. A sovereign state does not accept any external authority and establishes itself as the supreme source of authority within a well-defined territory. As defined in classic terms, sovereignty is absolute, perpetual and inalienable. As such, it cannot be shared, limited or divided; sovereignty is not a question of degree.

It was in Western Europe where the Westphalian model of sovereign state was initially established. But the building of a few large states affirming their own sovereignty vis-à-vis other states resulted in several centuries of war-making between monarchies, weak democracies, and new dictatorships. Western Europe only achieved an equilibrium based on democracy, peace, and prosperity when, after the Second World War, it undertook the construction of a large empire based on military, commercial, economic, monetary, and political cooperation among states. European states have ceded powers previously under their sovereign jurisdiction to new institutions of imperial scope. At the same time, most of the larger states decentralize their authority in favor of smaller units. Further members of the European "club" have found in that membership a way to avoid the perils of nonviable independence and the new dictatorships that would likely arise in such an environment.

As has been discussed in this book, most of Asia, North America, and Russia have been unacquainted with the Westphalian model of sovereign states. Traditionally nondemocratic or newly democratic very large empires encompass most of the population in those continents. It was in large parts of former European colonies in Latin America, Africa and the Arab region where the West European model of sovereign states was replicated most faithfully. But upon gaining independence from colonial dominion, the populations of those regions lost the advantages of belonging to a more extensive area able to provide common security, open trade, and other large-scale services. Nowadays, the failure of a high number of states in those world regions seems unquestionable. Among the usual characteristics of many Latin American, African, and Arab would-be "states" there is a lack of control of the territory and population by the government, an inability to extract taxes and provide the most basic public goods and services, persistent violence and widespread crime, frequent interstate border conflicts, and ethnic civil wars.

If the most recent European experience – and the American one, before it – are of any exemplary value, the building of military and commercial large "empires" seems, therefore, to be a precondition for freedom, stability and progress in those areas that have been subject to never-ending processes of trial and error in the art of building nation–states. The Organization of American States, the Free Trade Agreement of the Americas, the African Union, the League of Arab States, and similar institutions have so far been revelations of intention and hope more than effective institutional networks. But only if tight "imperial"-sized networks of this sort are built and put into effect can the states and nations in those regions of the world find the opportunity to attain stable democracy, peace and prosperity.

References and further reading

Introduction

My own requirements for a serious piece of work in the social sciences was sketched and discussed in Josep M. Colomer *Political Science is Going Ahead (By Convoluted Ways). A Commentary on Giovanni Sartori* PS: Political Science and Politics, 37, 4, 2004, pp. 703–4.

1 Large empires

The concept of empire and its potential in the analysis of long term historical periods was discussed in the excellent book coauthored by an outstanding selection of historians and political scientists at the initiative of Maurice Duverger (ed.) *Le Concept d'Empire* Paris: Presses Universitaires de France, 1980. The only political science-oriented history of the forms of government in the world that goes beyond the last 200 years is the impressive, indispensable and irregular study by Samuel E. Finer *The History of Government from the Earliest Times* Oxford: Oxford University Press, 3 vol., 1997. There are interesting suggestions for further work in George E. Von der Muhll *Ancient Empires, Modern States, and the Study of Government* Annual Review of Political Science, 6, 2003, pp. 345–76. See also Michael Doyle *Empires* Ithaca, NY: Cornell University Press, 1986.

Data about empires in Table 1.1 are taken from four illuminating articles by Rein Taagepera *Size and Duration of Empires: Systematics of Size* and *Size and Duration of Empires: Growth–Decline Curves, 3000 to 600 BC* both in Social Science Research, 7, 1978, pp. 108–27 and 180–96, *Size and Duration of Empires: Growth–Decline Curves, 600 BC to 600 AD* Social Science History, 3 and 4, 1979, pp. 115–38; and *Expansion and Contraction Patterns of Large Polities: Context for Russia* International Studies Quarterly, 41, 1997, pp. 475–504 which are largely based on Colin McEvedy and Richard Jones (eds) *The Atlas of World Population History* Harmondsworth, Middlesex, UK: Penguin, 1978, which has also been consulted.

2 Sovereign states

Two generations of political scientists ago, some fundamental discussion was collected by S. N. Eisendstadt and Stein Rokkan (eds) *Building States and Nations* Beverly Hills–London: Sage, 2 vol., 1973. As they were embedded in the "modernization" paradigm, the editors acknowledged they had been incapable of "developing a general theoretical structure for comparisons across all regions of the world," but remarked on "the uniqueness of the Western experience of state formation and nation-building" and its inappropriateness for the "Third World;" specifically for Africa, for instance, "nation-building in the European style was a luxury when not a catastrophe." See also Stein Rokkan and Derek W. Urwin (eds) *Economy, Territory, Identity: Politics of West European Peripheries* London: Sage, 1983.

More recently, a masterful historical survey of the modern states is given by Martin L. Van Creveld *The Rise and Decline of the State* Cambridge: Cambridge University Press, 1999.

Other enlightening studies on the formation of early states include William Doyle *The Old European Order 1660–1800* Oxford–New York: Oxford University Press, 1978; Charles Tilly (ed.) *The Formation of National States in Western Europe* Princeton: Princeton University Press, 1975; Hendrik Spruyt *The Sovereign State and Its Competitors* Princeton: Princeton University Press, 1994; and Philip Bobbitt *The Shield of Achilles. War, Peace, and the Course of History* New York: Alfred Knopf, 2002.

The importance of initial violence, force and coercion in building a state that may deliver efficient public goods at only a further stage has been stressed by Margaret Levi *Consent, Dissent and Patriotism* New York: Cambridge University Press, 1997; Robert H. Bates *Prosperity and Violence: The Political Economy of Development*, New York: W. W. Norton, 2001; and Charles Tilly and Sidney Tarrow *Contentious Politics* Boulder, CO: Paradigm 2006.

My point on the different labor-intensive and technology-intensive investments that are required at different scales for building a state bureaucracy (which should probably be further developed), is based on a comparison of some insights by William A. Niskanen *Bureaucracy and Public Economics* Aldershot, UK: Edward Elgar, 1994, and Oliver Williamson *The Economic Institutions of Capitalism* New York: The Free Press, 1985. A simple test should show that in failing or weak states with tiny bureaucracies, the proportion of public expenditure in personnel is higher than in robust states with more extensive bureaucracies, thus making small, labor-intensive bureaucracies more socially inefficient than large, technology-intensive ones.

The model of the USA, not as a sovereign state but a "compound republic," has been elaborated, among others, by Vincent Ostrom *The Political Theory of a Compound Republic: Designing the American Experiment* Lincoln: University of Nebraska Press, 1987. For a critique of the export and failure of the state model beyond Europe see, for instance, Bertrand Badie *L'état Importé. Essai sur l'Occidentalisation de l'Ordre Politique* Paris: Fayard, 1992. The failure of statehood as an explanation for social disorder and economic stagnation is not, however, very frequent and, when used, it is typically within a teleological framework by which state building is presented as the only possible model for non-European countries; see Francis Fukuyama *State-Building: Governance and World Order in the Twenty-first Century* Ithaca, NY: Cornell University Press, 2004.

The historical list of states in Table 2.1 is partly based on data from Kristian S. Gleditsch and Michael D. Ward *System Membership Case Description List* (available at weber.ucsd.edu/~kgledits) and the *Correlates of War* project at the University of Michigan (available at www.correlatesofwar.org). A good collection of cases of states in process of separation can be found in Tozun Bahcheli, Barry Bartmann and Henry Srebrnik (eds) *De Facto States. The Quest for Sovereignty* London and New York: Routledge 2004. The mentioned World Bank LICUS initiative reports on fragile states can be found at www.worldbank.com/operations/licus; and for the British government in *Investing in Prevention: An International Strategy to Manage Risks of Instability and Improve Crisis Response* London: Prime Minister's Strategy Unit, 2005. Other periodical reports dealing with similar issues come from the Organization for Economic Cooperation and Development's *The Fragile States Group*, available at www.oecd.org/dac/fragilestates; Daniel C. Esty, Jack A. Goldstone, Ted Robert Gurr *et al. State Failure Task Force Reports* CIA's Directorate of Intelligence, Phase III Findings, 2000; and the Fund for Peace and Foreign Policy *The Failed States Index* Foreign Policy, July–August 2005.

3 Small nations and 4 Nation building and deconstructing

There are several measurements of the degrees of ethnic heterogeneity in contemporary states as combinations of racial, language and religious groupings, including Tatu Vanhanen *Domestic Ethnic Conflict and Ethnic Nepotism: A Comparative Analysis* Journal of Peace Research, **36**, 1, 1999, pp. 55–73; Alberto Alesina, Arnaud Devleeschauwer, William Easterly, Sergio Kurlat and Romain Wacziarg *Fractionalization*, and James D. Fearon *Ethnic and Cultural Diversity by Country* both in Journal of Economic Growth, **8**, **2**, 2003, pp. 155–94 and 195–222. In the first four chapters of this book, in addition to the sources mentioned, data have been completed with those provided by the United Nations, the World Bank, Wikipedia and other standard sources.

5 Military alliances

The so-called "military revolution" of the sixtenth century was first studied by Michael Roberts, followed by Geoffrey Parker's rejoinder, as can be seen in the compilation by Clifford J. Rogers (ed.) *The Military Revolution Debate: Readings on the Military Transformation of Early Modern Europe* Boulder, Co.: Westview Press, 1995; an encompassing panorama of technological changes in warfare is given by Martin L. Van Creveld *Technology and War. From 2000 BC to the Present* New York: The Free Press, 1991. The thesis that modern states developed and expanded under the pressure of the increasing costs of war-making has been elaborated by a number of social historians led by Charles Tilly; see, in particular, Tilly *War Making and State Making as Organized Crime*, in Peter Evans, Dietrich Rueschemeyer, and Theda Scokpol (eds.) *Bringing the State Back In* Cambridge–New York: Cambridge University Press, 1985.

Historical data on interstate wars are compiled in Tilly *Coercion, Capital, and European States, AD 990–1990* Oxford: Blackwell, 1990, based on the annual survey of Ruth Leger Sivard *World Military and Social Expenditures* Washington, DC: World Priorities (published since 1974), and Jack Levy *War in the Modern Great Power System, 1495–1975* Lexington, University Press of Kentucky, 1983. For the account of issues that generated wars, see Kalevi J. Holsti *Peace and War: Armed Conflicts and International Order, 1648–1989*, Cambridge–New York: Cambridge University Press, 1991. My numerical calculations are based on data on troops, weapons and military expenditure provided by the Correlates of War project, mentioned above, and the Stockholm International Peace Research Institute (available at www.sipri.org).

The official doctrine promoting a more active role of the USA in spreading freedom and democracy in the world was formally presented in the document *The National Security Strategy of the United States of America* Washington, DC: White House, September 2002. A more propagandistic version is in Natan Sharansky *The Case for Democracy: Power of Freedom to Overcome Tyranny and Terror* Washington DC: Public Affairs, 2004. Bill Clinton's statement was at the 1994 State of the Union address. Condoleezza Rice's statement was quoted in The New York Times, 21 June 2005. There is, of course, a lot of discussion about whether all this implies more or less unilateralism or multilateralism in foreign policy and international relations, including the well-known pamphlet by Robert Kagan *Of Paradise and Power: America and Europe in the New World Order* New York: Alfred Knopf, 2003. For a contribution from a historical perspective by a non-American born author, see Niall Ferguson *Colossus: The Price of America's Empire* New York: Penguin, 2004. For a European perspective, see Timothy Garton Ash *Free World: America, Europe and the Surprising Future of the West* London: Allen Lane, 2004.

The thesis that democracies don't fight each other has been developed by, among many others, Michael W. Doyle *Ways of War and Peace* New York: W. W. Norton, 1997; Bruce Russett *The Democratic Peace: And Yet It Moves* International Security **19**, 4, 1995, pp. 164–75; Spencer R. Weart *Never at War: Why Democracies Will Not Fight Each Other* New Haven: Yale University Press, 1998; Bruce Bueno de Mesquita, James D. Morrow, Randolph M. Silverson and Alastair Smith *An Institutional Explanation of Democratic Peace* American Political Science Review, **93**, 4, 1999, pp. 791–807; and Dan Reiter and Allan C. Stam *Democracies at War* Princeton: Princeton University Press, 2002. The account of wars between democracies and dictatorships is based on R. J. Rummel *Death by Government* New Brunswick, NJ: Transaction, 1994.

6 Market agreements

The insightful argument about the economic viability of small nations in an international context of free trade was presented by David Friedman *A Theory of Size and Shape of Nations* Journal of Political Economy, **85**, 1977, pp. 59–77; and Donald Wittman *Nations and States: Mergers and Acquisitions; Dissolutions and Divorce* The American Economic Review, **81**, 2, 1991, pp. 126–9; and *The Wealth and Size of Nations* Journal of Conflict Resolution, **44**, 6, 2000, pp. 868–84; and developed in a series of papers and articles partly merged in the book by Alberto Alesina and Enrico Spolaore *The Size of Nations* Cambridge, MA–London: The MIT Press, 2003.

Historical economic data have been found in the several volumes edited by M. Postan and H. J. Habakkuk (eds) *The Cambridge Economic History* Cambridge–New York: Cambridge University Press, 1965 ff.; and in the historical statistics compiled by Angus Maddison *The World Economy: Historical Statistics, 1–2001 AD* available at www.eco.rug.nl/~Maddison. Updated information on international trade and on trade agreements can be found in the database of the World Trade Organization, available at www.wto.org. For historical and recent data on migrations

Department of Economic and Social Affairs, Population Division, Trends in Total Migration Stock. The 2003 Revision. New York: United Nations, 2003.

The seminal model for the analysis of the benefits and costs of currency areas was authored by the Nobel Prize awarded economist Robert A. Mundell *A Theory of Optimum Currency Areas* The American Economic Review, 51, 4, 1961, pp. 509–17. Mundell basically held that the larger the area the better and that, therefore, "the optimum currency area is the world," which has not been attained yet, as argued in this book. There has been much discussion on Mundell's model (and on why he was awarded the Nobel Prize); on the former issue, see, for example, Alberto Alesina and Robert J. Barro *Currency Unions* Quarterly Journal of Economics, 2002, pp. 409–36. There are good measurements of the trend towards continental-bloc concentration of international trade, based on data on exchanges between pairs of countries, in Jeffrey A. Frankel *Regional Trading Blocs in the World Economic System* Washington, DC: Institute for International Economics, 1997.

7   Linguas francas

The so-called "economic" approach to language, based on the analysis of benefits and costs of language choices for communication, can be found developed in Florian Coulmas *Language and Economy* Oxford–Cambridge: Blackwell, 1992. Good accounts of the question of the study of languages from several academic disciplines are provided in Joshua A. Fishman (ed.) *Handbook of Language and Ethnic Identity* New York–Oxford: Oxford University Press, 1999. Perhaps the only general history of languages is the one nicely written by Tore Janson *Speak. A Short History of Languages* New York–Oxford: Oxford University Press, 2002. For the history of old, very large languages, see Nicholas Ostler *Empires of the World. A Language History of the World* London: Harper Collins, 2005. For information about all languages of the present world, the indispensable source is Barbara E. Grimes *Ethnologue: Languages of the World* (15th ed.) Dallas: Summer Institute of Linguistics, 2005 (partly available under the editorship of Raymond G. Gordon, Jr., at www.sil.org/ethnologue). But very interesting information can also be found at www.yourDictionary.com.

The search for a world language has been discussed by Abram De Swaan *et al. The Emergent World Language System* International Political Science Review (special issue), **14**, 3, 1993, pp. 219–368. For English as international language, see, for instance, David Crystal *English as a Global Language* Cambridge–New York: Cambridge University Press, 1997. The calculations on the probabilities that multilingual individuals can understand each other were presented in my own work: Josep M. Colomer *To Translate or To Learn Languages? An Evaluation of Social Efficiency* International Journal of the Sociology of Language, **121**, 1996, pp. 181–97.

8   Small democracies

There was a preliminary attempt to evaluate the benefits and costs of size for democratic government, although rather abstract and tentative, by Robert A. Dahl and Edward R. Tufte *Size and Democracy* Stanford, CA: Stanford University Press, 1973, but surprisingly the subject is still heavily understudied. The quote from Montesquieu is from *L'Esprit des Lois,* 1748, vol. 1, book 8. The quotes regarding the evils of colonialism for the metropolis are from Adam Smith *The Wealth of Nations* 1776; Jeremy Bentham *Emancipate Your Colonies!* 1793, in *The Works of Jeremy Bentham* (ed. John Bowring), Edinburgh: William Tait, vol. 4, 1830; and *Rid Yourselves of Ultramaria* 1820–1822; and for Karl Marx, from Georges Haupt, Michael Lowy and Claudie Weill *Les Marxistes et La Question Nationale (1848–1914): Études et Textes* Paris: Maspero, 1974.

The calculations on the numbers of democracies, intermediate regimes and dictatorships in different country sizes and periods are based on data from *Polity IV: Political Regime Characteristics and Transitions, 1800–2003* (Monty G. Marshall, Keith Jaggers and Ted Robert Gurr, eds) (available at www.cidcm.umd.edu/inscr/polity) and R. D. Gastil and Adrian Karatnycky (eds), Freedom House *Freedom in the World: The Annual Survey of Political Rights and Civil Liberties* New Brunswick: Transaction, 1972–2005 (available at www.freedomhouse.org), partly collected also in my works: Josep M. Colomer *Political Institutions* New York–Oxford: Oxford University Press, 2001, and Josep M. Colomer *Comparative Constitutions* in the Oxford Handbook of Political Institutions (R. A. W. Rhodes, Sarah Binder and Bert Rockman, eds), New York–Oxford: Oxford University Press, 2006 (*Oxford Handbooks of Political Science* series, General Editor Robert Goodin). For other interesting relations between size, ethnic heterogeneity, political institutional regimes and democracy, see Marta Reynal-Querol *Ethnicity, Political Systems and Civil Wars* Journal of Conflict Resolution, **46**, 1, 2002, pp. 29–54, and Reynal *Does Democracy Preempt Civil Wars?* European Journal of Political Economy, **21**, 2, 2005, pp. 445–65.

9 Unity in diversity

The point that the European Union may not be "unique" was addressed, for instance, by Caporaso, in James Caporaso, Gary Marks, Andrew Moravcsik and Mark Pollack *Does the European Union Represent an N of 1?* European Community Studies Association Review, **10**, 3, 1997, pp. 1–2. The war motives in building large empires like the European one were remarked by Willian H. Riker in *The Development of American Federalism* Boston: Kluwer, 1987, and in *European Federalism: The Lessons of Past Experience* in Joachim J. Hesse and Vincent Wright (eds) *Federalizing Europe? The Costs, Benefits, and Preconditions of Federal Political Systems* Oxford: Oxford University Press, 1996.

The vision of the European Union as a new kind of empire was sketched by Robert Cooper *The Breaking of Nations. Order and Chaos in the Twenty-first Century* New York: Atlantic Monthly Press, 2003. It has been developed, parallel to the publication of the present book in Catalan and Spanish, by Jan Zielonka *Europe as Empire* Oxford: Oxford University Press, 2006. The increase of regional economic differentiation when large-scale integration develops, including the example of the automobile industry in a comparison between the European Union and the United States, is elaborated by Paul Krugman *Geography and Trade* Boston: MIT Press, 1991. Further discussion and empirical analysis of state and regional inequalities in Europe include Antoni Castells and Nuria Bosch (eds) *Desequilibrios Territoriales en España y Europa* Barcelona: Ariel, 1999. On languages in Europe, Miquel Siguan *L'Europa de les Llengües* Barcelona: Edicions 62, 1995 (see e-version in English at atotos.gksdesign.com). The quotes are from Voltaire *Langues* in *Dictionnaire Philosophique* 1763, and J. Gottlieb Fichte *Speeches to the German Nation* Speech 4, 1808.

10   Self-government à la carte

The implications of the building of the European Union and its expansion for territorial redistributions of power have been discussed in the collective book edited by Christopher K. Ansell and Giuseppe di Palma (eds) *Restructuring Territoriality. Europe and the United States Compared* Cambridge–New York: Cambridge University Press, 2004. See also Montserrat Guibernau *Nations Without States. Political Communities in a Global Age* Cambridge, UK–Malden, MA: Polity–Blackwell, 1999, and Michael Keating *The New Regionalism in Western Europe: Territorial Restructuring and Political Change* Cheltenham: Edward Elgar, 2000, among other works. Some discussion on the advantages of federalism for large-size democracy, including the cases of Germany and Switzerland, is included in Josep M. Colomer *Political Institutions* New York–Oxford: Oxford University Press, 2001. For crossing borders, J. Anderson, L. O'Dowd and T. M. Wilson (eds) *New Borders for a Changing Europe: Cross-border Co-operation and Governance* London: Frank Cass, 2003; Joan Vallvé *Cooperació Transfronterera a Europa/Cross-border Co-operation in Europe* Barcelona: Editorial Mediterrània, 2004.

11   A case of a failing nation–state

The most updated and encompassing study of the Spanish political system is Richard Gunther, José-Ramón Montero and Joan Botella *Democracy in Modern Spain* New Haven–London: Yale University Press, 2004. The solution "liberty and empire" was identified by the historian Jaume Vicens-Vives *Notícia de Catalunya* Barcelona: Destino, 1954. In contrast to Vicens's scholarship, however, the recent economic historiography has attained a new consensus around the idea that nineteenth century commercial protectionism was a bad business. For historical data, Leandro Prados de la Escosura *De Imperio a Nación. Crecimiento y Atraso Económico en España (1780–1930)* Madrid: Alianza, 1930; and Albert Carreras and Xavier Tafunell *Historia Económica de la España Contemporánea* Barcelona: Critica, 2004. On languages in Spain, see Miquel Siguan *España Plurilingüe* Madrid: Alianza, 1992.

I compared the polarization induced by the electoral system during the Spanish Second Republic in the 1930s and during the present monarchy in my chapter *Spain: From civil war to Proportional Representation* in Colomer (ed.) in *Handbook of Electoral System Choice* London–New York: Palgrave–Macmillan, 2004. For the relations between the decisions during the transition to democracy in the 1970s and the real working of democratic institutions, see Josep M. Colomer *Game Theory and the Transition to Democracy: the Spanish Model* Cheltenham: Edward Elgar, 1995; as well as my chapter *Spain and Portugal: Rule by Party Leadership*, in Colomer (ed.) *Political Institutions in Europe* (2nd ed.) London: Routledge, 2002.

12 Multilevel democracy

A general overview of the political institutions of the European Union is provided by Simon Hix *The Political System of the European Union* London–New York: Palgrave–Macmillan, 2006. For more data and analysis, I refer to my own works: Josep M. Colomer (ed.) *Political Institutions in Europe* (2nd ed.) London: Routledge, 2002 (updated 3rd edition forthcoming); Josep M Colomer *How Political Parties, Rather than Member-States, Are Building the European Union*, in Bernard Steunenberg (ed.) *Widening the European Union: The Politics of Institutional Change and Reform* London: Routledge, 2002; and Josep M Colomer *The Power of Political Parties in the Institutions of the European Union* in Peter Moser and Gerald Schneider (eds.) *Decision Rules in the European Union* London: Macmillan, 1998. The general information source for the European Union is www.europa.eu.int

Index